THE FAT LADY SINGS

THE FAT LADY SINGS
A Psychological Exploration of the Cultural Fat Complex and its Effects

Cheryl Fuller

Routledge
Taylor & Francis Group

LONDON AND NEW YORK

First published 2017 by Karnac Books Ltd.

Published 2018 by Routledge
2 Park Square, Milton Park, Abingdon, Oxon OX14 4RN
711 Third Avenue, New York, NY 10017, USA

Routledge is an imprint of the Taylor & Francis Group, an informa business

British Library Cataloguing in Publication Data

A C.I.P. for this book is available from the British Library

ISBN-13: 9781782204978 (pbk)

Typeset by Medlar Publishing Solutions Pvt Ltd, India

This book is dedicated to my husband, Neal Harkness, who loves me more than I thought anyone could, who listened to me fret about this and that, and who throughout it all remained calm and comforting.

To Pauline Salvucci, my best friend ever, who died before I finished, who listened and cried and laughed with me as I wrote it, who more than anyone I know understood what it is like to be fat, and who would so have loved to celebrate with me now.

And lastly to my analyst, Gary Astrachan, who listened to me, fought with me, challenged me to look deeper into myself, helped me to see the value in my wounded places and to find the courage to express myself.

Thank you for being with me.

CONTENTS

ACKNOWLEDGMENTS

Many people have helped me along the way with this book. For taking time to read and offer suggestions my deepest thanks to Karen Hanson, Ann Hyland, and Hadar Aviram. My cheerleaders in the Brainstorms Community—Kristie Helms, Valerie Bock, Mary Montgomery, Richard Lee, and Chris Worden—thank you for your support.

Special thanks to Janice MacDonald who read through several versions of the book, corrected errors, and generally cheered me along every bit of the way.

My consultant, Elizabeth Nelson at Pacifica Graduate Institute and of Winged Feat, helped me to shape my chapters into a more coherent whole and encouraged me to find a publisher.

An earlier version of Chapter One was published by *Spring Journal. Spring Journal Volume 91: Women's Voices*, October 2014. www.springjournalandbooks.com. It is included here with permission.

ABOUT THE AUTHOR

Cheryl Fuller, Ph.D. is a Jungian psychotherapist living on the coast of Maine. She has her doctorate in Jungian Studies and many years of study and training at various Jung institutes and in Jungian analysis. She brings over forty years of clinical experience, humor, and enthusiasm to the study of Jung, psychotherapy, feminism, and fat studies. She has a private practice for individuals in Maine and online.

The silent woman

Many years ago in Waterville, Maine there was a restaurant, The Silent Woman, with a huge sign visible from the highway. The sign depicted a decapitated woman serving refreshments on a tray—a headless woman performing her service function with the implication that this is perhaps the highest and best form of woman, woman without a voice.

Today, we see her still as the "headless fatty," a term coined by Charlotte Cooper (Cooper, 2007). When journalists run stories on television and in print about the evils of obesity, there she is, a fat, usually a very fat woman on the street or the beach or in some other public place. In such stories fat people are almost without exception shown without heads. The earlier headless woman came from a time when it was believed that women talked too much. A headless woman, therefore, would be silent and could go about her duties serving and taking care of men. But why today the Headless Fatty? Why are they headless? Because anyone who looks like this would/should be ashamed to have her face show? Because it allows the viewer to see her as an object and not a person? Judith Moore, author of *Fat Girl*, writes:

> The most shameful fat facts, and those facts most avoided when
> the fat or formerly fat write about fatness, are facts about the fat

body … What people do want to write about is weight loss and how to lose it. They want to write about self-esteem and how to gain it. (Moore, 2005, p. 174)

The Headless Fatty is our modern-day Silent Woman. Give her a voice and she will say things people do not want to hear.

* * *

For nearly all of my life thin people have been telling me what I should do to become thin like them. It gets old fast, having someone who has no idea what I have already tried, how many times I have tried, and no idea what it is like to be fat telling me what I should do to be thin, to be normal, to fit in, as if I hadn't already tried to do just that more times than I could count. For much of my life, I mutely tried hard, very hard to do what they said. Almost everything written or said about fat and being fat comes from people who themselves are not fat and likely have never been. We fat people are rarely consulted about what it is like to be fat, about how we eat and move and live our lives because we are not seen as credible, because we are not seen as reliable witnesses to our own experiences and lives. As Terry Tempest Williams wrote, "When silence is a choice, it is an unnerving presence. When silence is imposed, it is censorship" (Williams, 2012, p. 24). Now is the time for the fat lady to sing. And as Helene Cixous urges:

By writing her self, woman will return to the body which has been more than confiscated from her, which has been turned into the uncanny stranger on display-the ailing or dead figure, which so often turns out to be the nasty companion, the cause and location of inhibitions. Censor the body and you censor breath and speech at the same time. Write your self. Your body must be heard. Only then will the immense resources of the unconscious spring forth. (Cixous, 1976, p. 875)

This is my story, the story of a fat woman.

It is also a look at fat and our culture, about the fat complex our culture is gripped by and how to respond to it. It grows out of my life as a fat woman, my work as a psychotherapist, and my experience as a patient in analysis. Rooted in analytical psychology, it challenges the notion that it is the fat patient who must be changed to fit into a thin world.

I began this work taking the stance of the fat acceptance and Health At Every Size (HAES) movements on this question in opposing Marion Woodman and Susie Orbach, the major depth psychological voices in the field. From fat activists I took the view that the psychological and medical communities and others are all off the track in pathologising fat, seeing it as a pathological medical, psychological, and social phenomenon. Under the mantra of treatment and prevention, the conventional view is that fatness is a problem that requires a solution, that is, the physical reduction of the fat body, and the elimination of the potential for individuals to become fat. The activists certainly have a point, because fat is not in and of itself evidence of pathology, as is widely assumed. But when being fat intersects and occurs with the complexes Woodman explores, then fat symbolically becomes a visible manifestation of those complexes and the emotions they are associated with. For a fat person, for me, to be whole as I am, I have to come to terms with the body I have—embrace it, inhabit it, cherish it, live fully in it—and do the work of minimizing the negative effects of those complexes. The complexes are not unique to fat people, though being fat brings another dimension to them because of cultural stigma attached to it. This is a departure from Woodman, who sees fat as a symptom in the traditional sense, as indicative of something wrong.

The chapters following fall broadly into three parts:

In the first, you will learn what it is like to live as a fat person in everyday life. Giving voice to the Headless Fatty is an important piece of this work.

The second examines the so-called War on Obesity as an example of a cultural complex, how that complex shapes the way fat is treated in psychotherapy, including the classical Jungian approach to fat, as written by Marion Woodman. I will engage her theory using myself as a kind of single case study and critique her theory by exploring how it fits with my history and experience.

In the third part, through the lens of the cultural fat complex, I look at the experience of being fat as an ongoing trauma. I will then return to the consulting room with thoughts about how better to meet and work with the fat patient in psychotherapy.

Throughout I weave my personal experience as a fat woman, as an analysand, and as a psychotherapist in and out of a critical examination of fat and the cultural complex that grips us about appearance, weight, and conformity to an unattainable ideal.

A note on "fat" *vs.* "obese"—In groups of people who have been marginalized on the basis of race or sexual orientation, an important part of claiming agency is declaring the right to choose what members call themselves. Similarly it is the practice in the fat community to reclaim the term "fat" from the pool of epithets directed against us, as segments of the gay community have reclaimed "queer." Therefore in what follows, I generally use "fat" rather than "obese" except when quoting or referring to research reports.

CHAPTER ONE

Life in the panopticon

Panopticon:

1. An area where everything is visible.
2. A circular prison with cells distributed around a central surveillance station; proposed by Jeremy Bentham in 1791.
3. A prison so constructed that the inspector can see each of the prisoners at all times, without being seen.

I am a fat woman. I have been fat since I was five. As a young child, I used to hide from my uncle who would poke me and laugh and call me "Fatty" while singing "The Too Fat Polka"—how I hate that song. Too many times my mother told me I was "as big as the side of a house." From early on I felt the sting and shame of being too big, too much. The humiliation of being weighed in gym class. The blind date that told his friend, within my earshot, that I was a "dog." Knowing I was different and feeling shame for not being slender like other girls, like my mother. And being told too many times, "But you have such a pretty face" as if my body were an aesthetic crime.

An introvert, I am also shy, always a bit ill at ease in large groups or with strangers. Being fat only magnified that shyness. In my early thirties after years of dieting and battling against my weight, I tired of it all.

1

I could not do one more diet, spend one more day obsessing about what I could and could not eat, one more night going to bed feeling an utter failure because I was hungry, because I was losing so slowly or not at all. Perpetually being on a diet meant that my days were filled with obsessing about what I could eat, what was forbidden, mentally calculating the calorie count of every food. And as I slept, dreaming of banquets I could never enjoy. There was only one thing left that I could do—the hard work to stop hating my body, to become able to look at and feel myself without cringing or eviscerating myself with insults and criticism. Simply put I had to give up the endless and fruitless effort to starve my wayward body into submission. The work I did to learn not to loathe my fat body enabled me to go places, to meet people without constantly worrying about how they saw me. I learned a cheery, warm, and pleasant persona for public spaces, because somewhere inside I believed that if I made myself pleasant and easy to be around then at least I could avoid hearing the negative judgments about my body. I was careful to dress nicely, to try to act like I felt pretty. And as long as I didn't think about it, didn't start looking at myself from outside myself, I believed in my own magical powers and I could be out and about and forget about the shame I wear in my flesh. I learned to pull myself way inside my body, away from my skin, away from the surface where I could be hurt, and I could become this sparkling personality and be unaware of my physical self. I could be like the nymph Echo, a voice without a body. The price? Become a body condemned to echo what she hears but not speak her own experience. I could wrap myself in my invisibility cloak of charm and move through the world insulated from the judgments and scrutiny of others. In order to move around in the world, I had to protect myself this way or risk being crushed by the weight and sharpness of looks and judgments I encountered and the shame I pushed down inside. I had to maintain silence.

For almost all of my adult life, I have wanted desperately to find a reason for this fat I carry, some explanation that I could rest on. There had to be some reason that I have this body that everything around me tells me is wrong, is bad, is a mistake or mark of weakness and disease. At times I told myself it is all about biology and genetics, an inevitable outcome of being my father's daughter, like his sisters and mother, all of them fat women who lived long lives. There is comfort in that explanation because if the reason for my fat is genetic, then it is not my fault any more than my eye color or height is my fault; it is just the way I was made.

Other times I would fall to the other side of the coin and believe the cause lay in my troubled relationship with my mother. I read Hilda Bruch, Marion Woodman, Geneen Roth, Kim Chernin, and all those others who led me to believe that if I could just work my way through those issues, then everything would change and I would be normal, I would become thin and stay that way. So I talked and wrote endlessly about my mother and my relationship with her. I told the stories of my childhood with her so many times that they almost seemed no longer mine.

Then I read *Fat is a Feminist Issue* and once more it all became muddled, this time in feminist politics and the tyranny of the patriarchy. I began to consider again that maybe this fat body *is* my normal, maybe this is the body I am meant to have and that trying to make it smaller is to be in a constant state of war with myself. Without realizing it, I became part of the fat acceptance movement. Identity politics gave me a new way to experience my self and my fat. I could think about this body, my fat body, being the right one for me. I could connect myself with a primal round earthy feminine, an earlier and more generous version of beauty, fertility, and womanliness. If I did not press too hard nor look too deeply, I could see that. I dreamed of a fat woman with colored ribbons for hair who danced naked with delight in her own fleshy abundance. I painted her. There were even moments when I felt her.

But I could not escape the hatred for fat that was all around me. On the internet, where anyone can hide behind a pseudonym, trolls feel free to vent their fat hatred as in the following left in anonymous comments on various blogs:

> But fat really is gross and ugly. It's a sign of indulgence, lack of exercise, poor life choices. Yuck. I wouldn't date a fat person if we were the last two people on earth.

> The last thing we need is another whining class of victims. Most of the time, fat people are victims of only one thing: their own appetites.

> Fat people are ugly and they stink. I don't like looking at them. I like looking at athletic bodies, both male and female. They are works of art (and whoever defiles the body, defiles the soul). I like the beauty of such a bio-machine in motion. It is ART. I like the shadows cast by the muscles; I like

when I see the tendons push out the skin. When I see this, I want to go up to that person and strum the tendons like a violin. I don't see any of that with fat people. But I smell fat people when they spill over into my seat.

Read the comments to almost any article that relates to fat people, especially fat women, and the bile spills out. There seems to be no barrier to expressing such bigotry. And though it is usually unspoken, nearly every fat person has seen or heard enough similar judgment to be aware that any time she walks down the street, someone is thinking or saying things like that. Fat people swim in a sea of toxic prejudice.

It is a battle on multiple fronts, this trying to come to terms with, to understand and be conscious about fat. First is the battle with the prejudice and condemnation of the culture, the hatred and disgust directed at fat people. How do I make my way in a world in which my very body is seen as too much, as emblematic of appetite run amok? A world in which even strangers feel it is helpful to me to call my attention to my size and/or to offer "helpful" suggestions on what I should do to become smaller, to take up less of their precious space? A world in which any time I enter an airplane, I know that there are passengers already on board praying I won't take the seat next to them because I might encroach upon their space, because I might somehow touch them with the curse of my fat.

Then there is the battle within, the struggle to discern the meaning of my fat without taking on blame. How do I not feel crushed by the weight of blame for my own body, the blame that comes with the belief that all I had to do to be "normal" was to eat less and move more? The struggle is to find my way through the judgment and shame that blame brings with it.

Finally is the battle with the introjected judgments that surround me, that voice that echoes the judgments around me and attacks me viciously for being out of bounds, for being too much. Telling me, in every kind of entertainment I seek out, every advertisement to which I am exposed, every newspaper or magazine I read, every form of media I consume that bodies like mine are bad, take up too much space. That I am undisciplined, ugly, lazy, stupid. That my body is offensive.

Lester Spence, a African-American political scientist, writes about the freedom of being in "black space" where he can be fully himself, where he knows the people there have visceral understanding of what it is to be a black man, where there is a shared cultural background and where "I can, in those spaces, breathe" (Spence, "Black Space", n.d.).

Contrast this with what he calls "white spaces" where he must "consciously be aware of what I am saying, of who is around me, of what I am wearing, of what I am doing, of what others are saying and doing. In critical ways, I cannot let my guard down for a moment" (Spence).

There is nothing like Spence's black space for most of us who are fat except perhaps at gatherings of fat acceptance activists. There are few places where I can just breathe, not have to explain myself or watch myself or work to ignore the looks of disapproval. Places where I fit in, where I can be, do, and move without being subject to scrutiny and silent, or usually silent, judgment. It is only when I am at home, with the people who love me, or with my friends or family that I can approximate that kind of space, where I feel no need to excuse or pretend to agree with the general attitude about fat. Every place else is like Spence's "white space," space where my fat reveals what must be my shame, my laziness, my self-indulgence, my gluttony, my too-muchness. When my friend, my very fat friend died a few years ago, I heard people, people who were her friends, attributing her death to her weight and during the long days before her death, as she lay in the ICU on a respirator, some of those friends of hers said that maybe now, when she recovered, she would lose weight as if she were choosing to be fat. I imagine that morbid obesity is listed in her hospital records as a contributor to her death. The truth is that she died of a virulent infection she acquired in the hospital, a hospital with the worst infection rate in the state. The truth is that for years she received less than adequate medical care because her doctors saw fat and failed to see her illnesses or to treat her with dignity or listen to her respectfully.

It's not much space, fat space. It is a few rooms in the whole of my world where, like Lester Spence in black space, I can be fully myself. With a few people that I trust don't judge me or find me disgusting or believe my body is an indicator of my character or my health. When I am in thin space and I enter a room where there are other people, without thinking, I scan the room to see if there are other fat people there. To be the only fat person is to stand out in an uncomfortable way. I find relief when there is someone else as fat or fatter than I am.

If I am in thin space and I go out to eat with others, say for lunch during a workshop, I am aware of what everyone eats. Notice how often women apologize to each other for eating—"I didn't't eat breakfast so I need a big lunch." or "I should just have a salad."—there seems to be an unwritten rule that it is gauche to enjoy eating, to eat whatever and as much as one wants. So I am careful to eat sparingly and never have dessert. I don't feel free to eat freely, enthusiastically. I know if I have French fries with my sandwich, there will be little mental cluckings over that.

I don't go shopping with other women. We can't shop in the same stores. There is no store in my town where I can buy clothes. I can't exchange clothes with other women. None of my friends wears my size.

In thin space I am always on guard. Even as I work to maintain my cloak of invisibility, I am hyper-aware of my behavior—my voice, how I move. I made myself learn to walk lightly. I am vigilant. Always aware of the others. In thin space, I am thin-skinned.

Sometimes I am physically very self-conscious. At those times it is harder for me not to look at me from outside myself. I "see" myself when I think about going someplace new and outside of my fat space and I can be flooded with an uncomfortable sense of self-consciousness. I feel inhibited and reluctant to go. I make myself go, but it is an act of brute force and I am unable to "forget" about the judgments and looks that I am usually able to make myself oblivious to. At those times I can't find my invisibility cloak. I feel naked and exposed. How to be in thin space without being thin-skinned, without being angry, without my invisibility cloak? I cling to my tiny fat space. And try to breathe.

If I want to be perceived as compliant, I know how to present myself as the Good Fatty, the fat person who believes in the socially dominant viewpoint that her number one goal in life should be losing weight (Bias, 2014). All I have to do is talk about trying to lose weight, about my desire to be thin. I can say I have lost ten, or fifteen, or thirty pounds and I will be praised for my efforts, even if it is a lie. The Good Fatty is apologetic for being fat and is in a perpetual state of trying to become thin. The Good Fatty doesn't threaten thin people because she tells them she is engaged in the same struggle to subdue her body that they are. The Good Fatty is apologetic for her fat, as if she must ask forgiveness for committing an aesthetic crime with her too-muchness or must do penance for taking up too much space. She doesn't complain about the relative lack of variety in clothing available to her and accepts that she should wear shapeless cover-ups, preferably in dark colors. She accepts as just that she pays more for her clothing, health care, and seats on airplanes. Because she knows she deserves it. She accepts without protest the "helpful" advice and criticism she receives from others because she is trying to become better, to become thin. She swallows her anger because she knows it is all her fault, that she has failed, and is getting what she deserves.

No matter where I go or what I do, I am almost always surrounded by messages about the unacceptability of my body. The constant examination of the fat body by doctors, social workers, and psychiatrists, teachers, lay people, comedians, journalists, even First Lady Michelle Obama (Welsh, 2011), are in effect attempts to exert a societal discipline to make "docile bodies" (Foucault, 1995, p. 136). In the prison designed by Benthem, the panopticon, the power over the prisoners arose from their ignorance about whether they were being observed. The discipline came through their self-monitoring more than through external force. We fat people are meant to feel shame, to feel we are responsible for our weight. We internalize the judgments and endless indictments for our failure to have become slender, for being too lazy or hungry or weak to bring our wayward bodies under control. In this way we exert self-discipline over our bodies. As with the prisoners, monitoring is internalised and self-imposed.

Every time I have hidden my eating from others, or felt too self-conscious to eat in public something that I want, like dessert, or have avoided eating altogether, I have eaten the disgust others feel for my body. I eat their disgust and it becomes part of me. Every time I buy my clothes from designated retailers, ones who deign to carry clothing in my size and I accept that I should pay more for clothing generally of lower quality than is available in so-called normal stores, I am buying and wearing the revulsion designers of clothing feel for my folds of flesh and billowing hips and thighs (Cunningham, 2014; Krupnik, 2013). I worked at making myself be less self-conscious. I can use the word "fat" with ease. I am able to talk about the assaults, large and small, to my dignity that I encounter every time I leave my house. I can do all of these things. But I can never escape the panopticon (Foucault, 1980, p. 155). I am always under scrutiny. Underneath it all, underneath the work I did to stop hating myself, underneath the pleasant persona, way down under there where I look at myself from outside and see myself with others' eyes, in that place I judge myself as severely as they do, not always but it comes back more often than I like. And then I feel furious with myself for being fat. And with them for their disgust. Furious for being furious. I am furious. Underneath all of that I am furious. Which I dare not show. Fury. That I do not express. That I swallow.

This is the world I live in—constantly under scrutiny, contending with prejudice, experiencing on a daily basis the traumatic effects of being different, of not fitting in and yet striving to stay grounded in myself.

CHAPTER TWO

The war on obesity:
a cultural complex at work

From the late 70s through the 80s and into the 90s, though of course many women struggled with their weight, the overall climate was not as harsh and punitive about fat as it is today. Susie Orbach published *Fat is a Feminist Issue* in 1978. William Bennett and Joel Guerin published *The Dieter's Dilemma*, a book grounded in medical research, in 1983. Carol Shaw launched *Big Beautiful Woman* magazine in 1979. A flurry of books and pamphlets from what was called the Fat Liberation Movement began fat acceptance. All of these publications, and others, urged fat women to listen to their bodies, presented research showing that dieting is in fact a losing battle, one in which most will regain all weight lost and often more. The magazine gave fat women their first chance to see women like themselves modeling beautiful clothes, and even lingerie and bathing suits, images of women none of us ever saw in mainstream fashion magazines. It is no small matter to be able to see images in a glossy fashion magazine of fat women, women like me. By no means did these publications and others similar to them mean that there was no bias against fat or that it was a kind of Camelot for fat people, but there was nothing like a war being waged against fat and fat people like there is today. In the 90s something changed and any softening of the climate toward fat ended. By the beginning of this century war on fat was declared, a war that continues unabated. As Betty Meador tells us,

> The influence of the culture is so great that the individual internalizes its precepts and expectations to such an extent that they become an unconscious and pervasive influence in everyday life, hidden like the blood in our veins, but shaping our identity, opinions, and behavior. (Meador, 2004, p. 172)

In order to explore the development and intensity of what is now called the War on Obesity from a Jungian perspective, thus to explore what this means, we must turn to consider what complex is at work here. Jungians are familiar with complexes. A complex is an emotionally charged group of ideas or images. When an individual or group is in the grip of a complex, their vision is distorted by the ideas and images of the complex. A person caught in a complex has a "sore spot" which leads to behavior that is automatic and stereotypical. The same response appears in every triggering situation, whether it is appropriate and helpful or not.

In their book, *The Cultural Complex: Contemporary Jungian Perspectives on Psyche and Society*, Thomas Singer and Samuel Kimbles bring a new perspective on the psychological nature of conflicts between groups and cultures by introducing the concept of the cultural complex:

> Intense collective emotion is the hallmark of an activated cultural complex at the core of which is an archetypal pattern. Cultural complexes structure emotional experience and operate in the personal and collective psyche in much the same way as individual complexes, although their content might be quite different ... cultural complexes tend to be bipolar, so that when they are activated, the group ego or the individual ego of a group member becomes identified with one part of the unconscious cultural complex, while the other part is projected out onto the suitable hook of another group or one of its members. (Singer & Kimbles, 2004, p. 6)

Singer explains that cultural complexes can be recognized as follows:

1. They express themselves in powerful moods and repetitive behaviors. Highly charged emotional or affective reactivity is their calling card.

2. They resist our most heroic efforts to make them conscious and remain, for the most part, unconscious.

3. They accumulate experiences that validate their point of view and create a storehouse of self-affirming ancestral memories.

4. Personal and cultural complexes function in an involuntary, autonomous fashion and tend to affirm a simplistic point of view that replaces everyday ambiguity and uncertainty with fixed, often self-righteous, attitudes to the world.

5. In addition, personal and cultural complexes both have archetypal cores; that is, they express typically human attitudes and are rooted in primordial ideas about what is meaningful, making them very hard to resist, reflect upon, and discriminate. (Singer with Kaplinsky, 2010, p. 7)

Cultural complexes can be seen in issues of religious conflict, racism, homophobia, and in the Islamophobia so common since 9/11. In all of these instances, we see an "us vs. them" attitude at work. The scapegoat complex, so named by Sylvia Brinton Perera, and derived from the Yom Kippur ritual of the ancient Jews, thus is an integral part of the cultural complex. In the scapegoat ritual, two goats were chosen by lot. One was offered as a blood sacrifice in the temple and, in its death, atoned for the sins of the community. The other was sacrificed to Azazel and sent away into the wilderness carrying the sins of the people (Callan, 2004, p. 3).

The fat complex takes its most obvious form in the so-called "War on Obesity." Between 1980 and 2004, media attention to obesity increased exponentially, from sixty-two articles published in the Lexis-Nexis with "obesity" in the headings, lead paragraphs, or key terms in 1980, to over 6,500 in 2004 (Campos, Saguy, Ernsberger, Oliver, & Gaesser, 2006). In 1993 Anna Kirkland, searching on the term "obesity epidemic," found in a Lexis-Nexis search "exactly one hit; that number grows so explosively that by 2001, there are 101 hits and by 2004, 770 hits" (Lebesco, 2010, p. 75). And that was more than ten years ago. A similar search done today would yield thousands of hits. Using the search term "obesity epidemic 2015" under News on Google on 31 July 2015, over five million results are returned, this is but one indicator of the increasing dimension of the focus on obesity as an epidemic.

Every day we hear or read the terms "war on obesity" and "obesity epidemic." These terms are used without question or consideration of what they actually mean. Thinking critically about such terms and how they are employed, we start with a trenchant observation from Deborah Lupton:

> In and of itself, fat has no meaning. It is the specific historical, social and cultural context in which fatness is lived, experienced, portrayed and regulated which give it meaning, just as other bodily attributes or features such as skin or hair colour, youth and height take on certain meanings depending on their context. (Lupton, 2012, p. 3)

In the grip of the fat complex, either one belongs to the righteous group where rigid control of appetite is maintained, where dieting is the rule rather than the exception, where value is measured in Body Mass Index (BMI) and clothing size or one is consigned to the territory of the scapegoat to be targeted by the media, scrutinized by health professionals, subjected to ridicule, made to suffer for being too much, for taking up too much space. Fat people become the repository for the sins of the culture as a whole. Fat people are the sin-eaters.

Creating the enemy

In war, there must be an enemy dehumanized in a process that legitimizes the attack against him or her. In *Faces of the Enemy: Reflections of the Hostile Imagination*, Sam Keen explores the ways that propaganda in wars serves the purpose of dehumanizing those determined to be enemies. He demonstrates the same pattern in conflict after conflict. First we identify ourselves as victims. Then we blame, demonize and finally dehumanize our adversaries, thereby rationalizing our attacks on other human beings.

During war, the enemy is referred to in derogatory terms and ethnic slurs such as "gook" or "towelhead," to increase their difference from us. They are caricatured to show them as grotesque or in some way different from those we see around us every day. In the war on obesity, the enemy—fat people—is dehumanized, made other which legitimizes the discrimination and bias directed against us. As mentioned earlier, in news photographs, fat people most often have no faces at all. It is much easier to feel contempt for a faceless mass of flesh than it is for a person, a real person. There is no requirement for consent to be obtained for use of a photo of a person taken in a public space. We see photos all the time of people in public spaces such as athletic events, political rallies, or street scenes. But when the goal is to show a fat person, what we are shown is a person with no head. Curious about this phenomenon, I contacted a photographer who had taken headless fatty photos used in a statewide newspaper in Maine. I asked him about this practice of omitting heads of fat people in news stories. He replied that it is a "sensitivity thing ... Not showing heads gives the generic overweight person's look but is not showing, that X specifically, is a fat person. If there was a story about one specific person being fat, that would be different" (G. Degre, personal communication, 3 February 2014). Who really is this sensitivity for? The fat person in the photo, who is deprived of her individuality by removing her head? She already knows she is fat as she lives with that reality every day. Or is it to allow the viewer to see that person as an object rather than a human being? Perform a Google image search using search terms like "obese" or "fat" or "fat person" and you will see among the images at least a few that you have seen before in newspapers and magazines. These familiar images show fat people, often in ill-fitting clothes that reveal their rolls of fat and make them look awkward. They are rarely shown participating in active movement or doing anything that might show grace or ease. What you see in the headless people are bodies out of control for there is no head, no brain to take charge and reign in appetite. Despite the fact that the Rudd Center at the University of Connecticut has created a royalty free gallery of images of fat people with heads shown in ordinary life activities (UCONN Rudd Center for Food Policy and Obesity, 2015), these headless images remain the most commonly used. The Headless Fatty is without voice, without mind, able only to demonstrate the assumed consequences of appetite and gluttony. As CS Lewis wrote, "How can they meet us face to face till we have faces?" (Lewis, 1985, p. 294).

Moral panic

A number of writers (Smith, 2004) have characterized the war on obesity as a moral panic. Considering the characteristics of a moral panic, the so-called War on Obesity is obviously an example of one: "A moral panic occurs when a phenomenon, occurrence, individual, or group of people comes to be seen as a threat to social values and interests" (Cohen, 1973, p. 9). Moral panics consist of the following characteristics:

> Concern—There must be awareness that the behaviour of the group or category in question is likely to have a negative effect on society.
>
> Hostility—Hostility towards the group in question increases, and they become "folk devils". A clear division forms between "them" and "us".
>
> Consensus—Though concern does not have to be nationwide, there must be widespread acceptance that the group in question poses a very real threat to society. It is important at this stage that the "moral entrepreneurs" are vocal and the "folk devils" appear weak and disorganised.
>
> Disproportionality—The action taken is disproportionate to the actual threat posed by the accused group.
>
> Volatility—Moral panics are highly volatile and tend to disappear as quickly as they appeared due to a wane in public interest or news reports changing to another topic. (Goode, & Nachman, 1994, pp. 33–39).

In order to justify the panic and its war, the dominant group must come to see itself as threatened, as victims. Let's look at ways that the rhetoric of war, fear of disease, and morality have been employed to heighten fear about and negative reaction to fat and thus create the moral panic and support a "war" on obesity.

Medicalizing fat

Looking back to the last century, at its beginning, Lillian Russell was the major beauty icon, considered so beautiful that the American Beauty rose was so named to honor her. Yet, at the height of her beauty, Russell weighed 200 pounds and would certainly be considered obese by today's standards. It is difficult to imagine a woman of her size being hailed today as a beauty, much less an iconic beauty. Today we would see condemnation of using images of her as supporting obesity as happened recently when *Sports Illustrated* featured a plus-size model in their swimsuit edition (Stump, 2016).

Usage of the terms "obese" and "obesity" instead of "fat" lends a tone of medical authority to discourse about fat and fat people. Until very recently obesity was not considered a disease but in 2013, the American Medical Association board voted to classify obesity as one. The vote went against the conclusions of the association's Council on Science and Public Health:

> The council said that obesity should not be considered a disease mainly because the measure usually used to define obesity, the body mass index, is simplistic and flawed ...
>
> Those arguing against it [the classification] say that there are no specific symptoms associated with it and that it is more a risk factor for other conditions than a disease in its own right. (Pollack, 2013)

Pressure for this classification likely came from pharmaceutical companies and bariatric surgeons and other groups with an economic interest in gaining support for coverage of this "disease" by health insurance. One obesity researcher said in an interview with Rebecca Weinstein:

> ... there are several important implications of this decision. Classifying obesity as a disease, or a health condition that may be, at least in part, due to circumstances beyond an individual's control, will open up the discussion to address it seriously and to persistently pursue all potential treatment options. It will help to overcome that barrier of blame and shame that currently occurs in the medical examination room. It will also force health insurance companies to consider covering its treatment. Additionally, treating it in a formal and standardized way will help evaluate and improve current standards of care. Lastly, classifying obesity as a disease will eventually create a medical support system for the treatment of obesity, which will, importantly, educate the public and put an end to the quackery that preys on obese individuals who are trying to lose weight every day. (Weinstein, 2014, pp. 104–105)

Her comment sounds reasonable until one considers that it classifies anyone above a certain BMI as diseased regardless of his or her actual state of health. And it carries the assumption that being fat is something that should be treated, that is, changed. Under this way of viewing obesity, treating fat can readily take priority over diagnosing and treating medical conditions that may or may not be related at all to weight.

In the imagination of ordinary people, terms like "morbid obesity" seem to be scientifically derived and based on research or medical knowledge. Following the World Health Organization's definitions, a person is obese if her Body Mass Index (BMI), which is weight in kilograms divided by the square of height in meters, is greater than 30 kg/m². But what does BMI mean? BMI was never intended as a measure of individual fatness or health as it is a population statistic. This is but one of a number of problems using it to define obesity (Tomiyama, Hunger, Nguyen-Cuu, & Wells, 2016). Its chief virtue is that it is a simple measure and relatively easy to calculate.

Scott and Law introduced the term "morbid obesity" in papers published in 1969 and 1970. In the latter article they described it:

> When an obese individual attains the gargantuan level of the fat man or fat woman in the circus and maintains this degree of massive obesity for many years, we believe the adjective morbid should be added to emphasize the serious health implications and severe, life-shortening hazards of such grotesque accumulations of fat. The social, economic, psychologic, and psychiatric aspects of massive obesity also have enormous importance for the individual who fits into this unfortunate category. (Scott, Sandstead, Lanier, & Younger, 1970, p. 770)

and in the earlier article defined it as:

> … any person whose weight has reached a level two to three or more times his ideal weight and who has maintained this level of obesity for five years or more despite efforts by himself, family, friends, and physicians to bring about effective and sustained reduction of weight to medically acceptable standards. (Scott & Law, 1969, p. 247)

Where is the data to support this? Note how vague and ill-defined the terms used to determine what "morbid obesity" is and the use of pejorative words like "gargantuan" and "grotesque," neither of which has any objective measure. What is "ideal weight"? How is this determined? This is the definition of ideal body weight, as given in the medical dictionary: "ideal body weight (IBW)—a weight that is believed to be maximally healthful for a person, based chiefly on height but modified by factors such as gender, age, build, and degree of muscular development" (Medilexicon, 2015). Trying to find solid data behind these terms immediately takes us down the rabbit hole into Wonderland.

It is also argued by some that because "obese" is a medical term it is somehow less stigmatizing and insulting to refer to a person as "obese" rather than as "fat." Yet, research shows otherwise. In a study examining whether the terms "obese people" *vs.* "fat people" impact evaluations of a target group, Vartanian found:

> Compared to fat people, obese people were rated as less favorable and as more disgusting. In addition, participants saw themselves as being less similar to obese people than to fat people, and as less likely to become an obese person than a fat person.
>
> ... Overall, the term "obese people" evokes stronger negative evaluations than the term "fat people." Researchers investigating weight bias should be aware that the specific terms used to refer to overweight and obese people can impact study outcomes and interpretations. (Vartanian, 2010, p. 197)

In support of the project of a "War on Obesity" we have an enemy—obese people who are wholly other, seen without faces and viewed as disgusting and out of control and suffering from a medical problem, thereby marking them as pathological.

Classifying obesity as a disease opens the door to medicalizing what is a human characteristic like height. Weight is commonly determined to be seventy to eighty percent heritable, second only to height. Though there are diseases associated with height, we do not speak of people being "overtall" nor do we suggest that parents work to somehow keep their children's height to some ill-defined "healthy height." But medicalizing weight makes it possible to begin to decry "the obesity epidemic," taking the language of public health to create a sense of emergency, which the moral panic needs to feed itself. When we hear "epidemic" we most commonly think of diseases like influenza or Ebola or measles with visions of many people dying, often terrible deaths. Indeed the common dictionary definition of epidemic is a disease affecting many persons at the same time, and spreading from person to person. A moment's thought leads anyone to see that certainly fat does not fit the criteria of this common definition. What we have with the "obesity epidemic" is a different kind of epidemic, what Borero (Borero, 2012, pp. 119–120) terms a postmodern epidemic. Unlike traditional epidemics of the past, in the case of obesity, there is no identified patho-gen, actually without any readily identified pathological basis or cause at all. In fact Morton Downey has identified at least 104 different causes of obesity from reports of research studies (Downey, 2015). Despite this, declaring an epidemic, even in the absence of anything resembling the common public health definition of epidemic, raises the alarm level and intensifies the moral panic and adds justification to a declaration of war on obesity.

In the War on Obesity, the enemy has been identified and dehuman-ized. Remembering that a moral panic is an intense feeling expressed in a population about an issue that appears to threaten the social order, what remains is to identify the threat to social order.

While no pathogen has been found as the cause for obesity, even so several researchers have attempted to identify obesity as contagious. The best known of these studies is one done by Christakis and Fowler in 2007. Published in the *New England Journal of Medicine*, they purported to demonstrate that obesity is socially contagious (Christakis & Fowler, 2007). News reports about the study spread widely. As reported in the *New York Times*:

> Obesity can spread from person to person, much like a virus, researchers are reporting today. When a person gains weight, close friends tend to gain weight, too.
>
> Their study, published in the New England Journal of Medicine, involved a detailed analysis of a large social network of 12,067 people who had been closely followed for 32 years, from 1971 until 2003. The investigators knew who was friends with whom, as well as who was a spouse or sibling or neighbor, and they knew how much each person weighed at various times over three decades. That let them examine what happened over the years as some indi-viduals became obese. Did their friends also become obese? Did family members or neighbors?
>
> The answer, the researchers report, was that people were most likely to become obese when a friend became obese. That increased a person's chances of becoming obese by 57 percent.
>
> There was no effect when a neighbor gained or lost weight, however, and family members had less influence than friends.
>
> Proximity did not seem to matter: the influence of the friend remained even if the friend was hundreds of miles away. And the

greatest influence of all was between mutual close friends. There, if one became obese, the odds of the other becoming obese were nearly tripled. (Kolata, 2007)

Time begins its report on the study this way:

> Wondering why your waistline is expanding? Have a look at those of your friends. Your close friends can influence your weight even more than genes or your family members, according to new research appearing in the July 26 issue of *The New England Journal of Medicine*. The study's authors suggest that obesity isn't just spreading; rather, it may be contagious between people, like a common cold. (Blue, 2007)

Look at the comparison—contagious "like the common cold"—and we all know how contagious that is. So no one is safe from this epidemic.

The social contagion theory was certainly itself contagious and spread widely before it came under scrutiny and was debunked. First Russell Lyons, a mathematician, attempted to publish a critique of the statistical methods Christakis employed by demonstrating that the conclusions were unsupportable. His work was rejected by multiple journals but was finally published in the journal *Statistics, Politics, and Policy*. But the damage had already been done as Christakis and others favoring a social contagion theory had gained a great deal of popular attention, not surprising given the discourse most supported by the cultural complex and its War on Obesity. There has been very little coverage of the important work Lyons and others have done refuting the theory of social contagion (Johns, 2011).

The social contagion theory is one of several theories feeding public alarm about obesity. Another is that obesity imposes a significant and ultimately intolerable cost burden on the society in high medical cost. Any medical problem a fat person develops is directly or indirectly attributed to being fat. Thus any medical expenses incurred by fat people appear to be attributable to their weight rather than other factors. Cost is a potent factor for arousing people's fears and thus is used again and again as one of the reasons for fighting this war. The diet industry profits hugely from the panic about fat. Current estimates are that spending on dieting and weight loss products surpassed $61 billion in 2014 and no doubt continue to rise (Weight Loss Statistics, n.d.).

In 2004 a paper from the Center for Disease Control reported that obesity caused 400,000 deaths in 2000, up from 300,000 a decade earlier, making it the second leading cause of preventable death behind cigarette smoking. Further the paper stated that if those trends continued, obesity would overtake smoking and become the leading cause of preventable death by 2005, with the toll surpassing 500,000 deaths annually (CaliforniaHealthline, 2004). The paper has since been removed from the CDC site. Katherine Flegal, an epidemiologist with National Center for Health Statistics, took issue with the paper, reporting that statistical flaws in the analysis of the data led to an overestimate of mortality of at least eighteen percent. Her group then did their own study and found:

> obesity and extreme obesity cause about 112,000 deaths per year, but being overweight was found to prevent about 86,000 deaths annually. Based on those figures, the net U.S. death toll from excess weight is 26,000 per year. By contrast, researchers found that being underweight results in 34,000 deaths per year. (Kaiser Health News, 2009)

Despite Flegal's work, reports in the media continue to use the very alarm statistics about deaths that she disproved. Again, her work has gotten far less attention than the original report because her work also looks at what is called the "Obesity Paradox"—that at extreme ends of weight distribution, both high and low, mortality is higher than expected but that those classified as "overweight" in fact have lower mortality (Kolata, 2005). There are many studies that attempt to disprove this paradox, so far without success. In a survey article by Hainer and Aldhoon-Hainerova, an advantage was shown for those who are obese or overweight in thirteen different serious medical conditions (Hainer & Aldhoon-Hainerová, 2013). Yet any finding that shows some advantage to fat is put under the "obesity paradox" because these findings are seen as suspicious and never as an advantage (Hughes, 2013). What is important here is that those studies receive very little attention in the media because they do not support the War on Obesity narrative, in much the same way that information about Islam as practiced by the vast majority of American Muslims does not fit the narrative of Islamophobia with its fears of imposition of sharia law and terrorism.

Yet another scare mongering alarm came in 2002 from William Klish of Texas Children's Hospital who told the Houston Chronicle that if the "epidemic" of "childhood obesity" was not checked, "for the first time in a century, children will be looking forward to a shorter life expectancy than their parents" (The Center for Consumer Freedom, 2005).

Three years later, the *New England Journal of Medicine* published a study by authors well known for their anti-obesity activism attempted to support Klish's statement. When challenged, they and Klish later acknowledged their statements were based on "intuition" rather than facts. But this admission came too late. Even now, ten years after the NEJM article and its retraction, this alarming notion that we are seeing the first generation whose life expectancy is less than their parents persists. You can find it in an article from the liberal site, ThinkProgress dated 2012 (ThinkProgress, 2012) and one from 2014 on overweight in children on the website the American Heart Association (American Heart Association, 2014). There are many others found readily in a Google search. All of this despite the reality that life expectancy continues to increase and the admission that the prediction was made up in the first place. It serves the moral panic, it works as a weapon in the war, and therefore it survives.

Obesity as societal threat

Capitalizing on the fears of terrorism, in the years since 9/11, both a U.S. Secretary of Health and Human Services and a Surgeon General of the U.S. have conflated obesity with terrorism. The first, Sec. Tommy Thompson just after 9/11 urged all Americans to lose ten pounds "as a patriotic gesture" (Rosenblatt, 2001). In 2006, Richard Carmona frankly connected obesity with terrorism, declaring, "Obesity is the terror within ... Unless we do something about it, the magnitude of the dilemma will dwarf 9–11 or any other terrorist attempt" (Pace, 2006). This calls forth images like those in film "WALL-E" with its legions of inert fat people.

Abigail Saguy offers this compelling description of effects of the moral panic we call the War on Obesity:

> The alleged obesity epidemic is seen as a symptom of a wide range of issues, including moral laxity, corporate greed, and addiction ...
> In the context of airplane travel, thin people are described as victimized by heavier travelers ... Reports on the economic costs of obesity paint the nonfat as victims, in that they are unfairly burdened with the cost of fat people's unhealthy lifestyles ...

> Economic analyses suggest that there are many institutional and social structural factors contributing to higher spending on health care in the United States over time and as compared to other industrialized democratic nations, including the higher incomes of medical professionals and expensive new technologies … It is easier to blame fat people for bankrupting society because of their self-indulgent ways. (Saguy, 2012, pp. 22–23)

In other words, fat people are fat because they are lazy, self-indulgent, lack discipline and cause problems not only for themselves but also for those around them and for the society at large. Hence, they deserve condemnation and any measures possible to reduce their numbers, to get them to be like thin people.

Fat as a moral issue

Not only has fat been medicalized into "obesity," it is also seen as a moral issue. Gluttony and sloth are counted among the Seven Deadly Sins. The Seven Deadly Sins, also known as the capital vices or cardinal sins, is a classification of vices rooted in early Christianity. To be fat is to be identified as gluttonous and slothful, guilty of two of the seven deadly sins as well as being emblematic of pathology, both psychological and physical. Francine Prose writes:

> our fixation on health, our quasi-obscene fascination with illness and death, and our fond, impossible hope that diet and exercise will enable us to live forever have demonized eating in general and overeating in particular. Health consciousness and a culture fixated on death have transformed gluttony from a sin that leads to other sins into an illness that leads to other illnesses. (Prose, 2003, p. 4)

Whereas these were once sins against God, as religion now has less direct power, the sin remains but now is secularized:

> … an affront to prevailing standards of beauty and health rather than an offense against God, the wages of sin have changed and now involve a version of hell on earth: the pity, contempt, and distaste of one's fellow mortals. What makes the glutton's penance all the more public and cruel is that gluttony is the only sin whose

effects (in the absence of that rare and fortunate metabolism that permits the fruits of sin to remain hidden) are visible, written on the body. Unlike, say, the slothful, who can, if they wish, manage to appear alert and awake, the modern glutton pays for and displays transgression by violating the esthetic norms of a society that places an extreme and even potentially dangerous emphasis on fitness and thinness. (Prose, 2003, p. 5)

Disregarding her questionable linking of gluttony and weight, the fat body is seen as emblematic of a failure of will, an indication of weak character, poor discipline, self-indulgence and greed. In response to efforts to counter fat shaming and bias, Fumento declares shaming and prejudice to be "a helpful and healthful prejudice for society to have because it is a 'prejudice against overeating and what used to be called laziness'" (Saguy, 2012, p. 41).

A colleague who studies religious violence tells me that ISIS and the new "caliphate" has recently put out the second issue of its English language magazine Dabiq, which contains the following account of a hadith or tradition of the Prophet:

> On the authority of 'Imrān Ibn Husayn (radiyallāhu 'anhumā) who stated that Allah's Messenger (sallallāhu 'alayhi wa sallam) said: "The best of my Ummah are those of my generation, and then those who follow after them, and then those who follow after them." 'Imrān said: "I do not remember whether he mentioned two or three generations after his generation." Then the Prophet added, "There will come after you, people who will bear witness without being asked to do so, and will be treacherous and untrustworthy, and they will vow and never fulfill their vows, and obesity will appear among them." (Cameron, Charles, personal communication, 6 September 2014)

Here is an identification of fat people as treacherous and untrustworthy, with fat as the marker for their faithlessness.

In the Christian context, there are a number of faith-based diet programs. One of these, The Lord's Table, describes its program:

> This 60-Day interactive course will teach you to enjoy a newfound relationship with the Lord. You will find freedom from the sin of

gluttony, by learning to follow biblical and practical ways, as you
daily proceed through this course. (The Lord's Table, n.d.)

Perhaps the most popular of these programs, the Weigh Down Ministry,
asserts fatness is a symptom of a faith crisis: overweight people have
mistaken a spiritual emptiness for a hunger for food. In these programs,
fat is a marker for the sin of gluttony and dieting is presented as the
way back into good relationship with Jesus and God. There is at least
one multifaith weight loss group as well: "a group of Muslim and Jew-
ish women in Brookline, Massachusetts who attend weekly meetings
to discuss 'the universal theme of weight-loss support', a group called
Slim Peace" (Hammerman, 2013).

In Dante's vision of Purgatory, the sixth terrace is where the gluttons are found. And the penance for gluttony is starvation. Think of
the medically supervised diet programs that disallow food per se and
substitute instead various shakes and bars and a daily calorie allotment
of 800 calories, well below what is considered necessary to maintain
adult health. In other words, these programs are supervised starvation,
the treatment earned by sinful fat people.

How often have you heard someone say she was "bad" today for
having eaten some food commonly deemed not healthy? Or confessed
guilt to having eaten some forbidden food and promising to do better the next day? On television reality series about cooking, the con-
testant emphasising "healthy" foods almost always loses because their
food celebrates not taste or delight but food as medicine and as virtue.
Prose writes:

> if you're overweight the last thing it seems to mean is that you
> have a passion for the tastes and flavors of food. Yet, for all its
> abhorrence of tiny weight gains and minuscule accretions of body
> fat, the culture is fixated on identifying the trendiest restaurant and
> the newest exotic ingredient. What results is often the phenome-
> non of rich, thin, young people eating tiny and absurdly expensive
> portions, or worse, of young women whose understandable dif-
> ficulty in interpreting the conflicting messages dispatched by the
> larger society contributes to the development of a host of common
> eating disorders. What's generally agreed upon now (at least in the
> popular imagination) is that the compulsive eaters, the modern-
> day gluttons, have some outstanding "issues" involving low self-
> esteem or past abuse, some bottomless void they are trying to fill by

binging on massive infusions of unhealthy, fattening food. (Prose,
2003, pp. 11–12)

These conflicting messages about food can readily be seen in the pages
of women's magazines like *Redbook* or *Woman's Day*. For example,
February always brings the diet that will give the reader the body she
wants to have by the time summer and bathing suit season comes. But it
is also the month of Valentine's Day, so much associated with chocolate
and foods to express love. Right next to the diet articles there will be
photographs of amazing desserts, calorie dense desserts that would
never be included on the diet plans in the pages of the same magazine.
Food articles in these magazines are lovingly and lushly styled and photographed, carefully designed to entice readers to prepare them. I have
long thought they are the food equivalent of pornography. Magazines
specifically focused on food and cooking, like *Bon Appetit* or *Saveur*, are
aimed at a high-end audience, the same group Prose cites above seeking
out the next trendy restaurant. Sin and seduction on every page.

At revival meetings held by evangelical Christians a high premium
is placed on what is called witnessing or testifying, declaring to the
group that in Jesus they have found salvation and their lives have
changed. Meetings of weight loss groups often have this same character.
Members declare how their lives have been changed by following the
program, using language not too dissimilar from the language of born
again Christians. When a member fails to show a weight loss, there is
an implied expectation that the member show contrition, acknowledge
her sin and vow to do better by following the program more carefully
and stringently.

That there are gluttonous thin people and slothful thin people
matters not at all as they do not wear their sins as fat people appear to.
The operative assumption seems to be that slender people are slender
because the ways they eat and exercise are the right ways to maintain
their body size and therefore they possess virtue. This means that fat
people must eat differently or different foods and not exercise because
otherwise they too would be slender. This assumption is fixed and
seemingly unchangeable. This is the essence of thin privilege.

Thin privilege

The notion of privilege has become a useful concept when exploring
differences among groups. Broadly, privilege is unearned benefits given

to people who fit into a particular group. Think of the benefit that flows to whites or males simply by virtue of skin color or sex. To this we can add weight as being thin also conveys privilege.

Privilege is not a consciously held or adopted attitude. Indeed the person carrying privilege, whether it be by virtue of sex, skin color, weight, sexual preference, or other categories of privilege, is almost always unaware of holding it. Thus the heterosexual person tends to see the world as heterosexual, to expect others to see it that way as well and only when attitudes and behaviors described as "hetero-normative" are pointed out to him or her is that privilege visible, able to come to consciousness. The Black Lives Matter movement and the LGBTQ movement bring to broader awareness issues of privilege vis a vis race and sexual orientation, awareness that most of us likely would not have without their efforts.

Thin privilege is discussed in fat acceptance communities and certainly underlies a great deal of the bias against fat. Linda Bacon writes of her own thin privilege:

> The word "privilege" is used to describe receiving unjust advantages at the expense of others. These advantages are often largely invisible—especially to those who enjoy them. For instance, I have what is called "thin privilege," a consequence of weight discrimination. Because I'm relatively thin, it's been easier for me to meet and get approval from other people. This has helped me make friends, find a life partner, develop professional contacts, and secure jobs. It also means I am treated with greater respect when I shop or eat in a restaurant. It means I have a larger choice of fashions at less expensive prices and never have to pay for more than one airline seat, making travel and its accompanying opportunities more accessible. I could go on for days listing the ways in which I have benefited from others' perception of my weight, but I believe these simple examples make the point. I can think of very little in my life that is untainted by "thin privilege." (Bacon, 2010)

Unlike Linda Bacon, most thin people are unaware that they carry thin privilege. And certainly they don't ask for it; this privilege comes to them simply by virtue of their size. It is an automatic assumption that thin people are thin because they do the right things and fat people are fat because they do not. And that thin people can save fat people by helping them to see the error of their ways, in much the same ways that evangelical Christians seek to bring the message of their faith to unbelievers. Fat people are surrounded by armies of missionaries for the gospel of thinness eager to tell us what we need to do to get right with ourselves and become thin like them. As Murray puts it:

> The fat body stands as a symbol of gluttonous obsessions, unmanaged desires and the failed self. In the midst of an historical epoch marked by a preoccupation with idealized body forms, and an eroticization of a slender bodily aesthetic, the fat body appears as a defiant blockage in a culture seduced by particularized notions of beauty and attractiveness. The body has come to be our visible representation to the world of our adherence to puritanistic lifestyle crusades, "correct" and "healthy" diets, exercise regimes and, most importantly, a reflection of the inner self. The body has come to be a representation of the "realized self". (Murray, 2004, p. 239)

How often have you heard that if a fat person would only eat 100 fewer calories each day, then by year's end she would weigh ten pounds less, as if the oft quoted 3,500 calories = one pound is absolutely and always true? Get those fat people to rein in their appetites, eat less, and move more, and then they too could be slender. This kind of thinking is what underlies efforts like a soda tax or the effort to ban super sized sodas that Mayor Bloomberg made in New York—because surely it is fat people, not thin people who overindulge in such foods. The assumption that banning soft drinks above a certain size was believed to offer a way to reduce calorie intake and thus reduce obesity (Engber, 2012). A rationale like this simply reflects beliefs about how fat people eat without much research data to support those beliefs. A related assumption is that obesity is more common among the poor than people with means and this is often attributed to overconsumption of fast food. But research does not support that assumption, though it is repeated again and again, as if thin people never eat fast food and fat people always do:

> A new national study of eating out and income shows that fast-food dining becomes more common as earnings increase from low to middle incomes, weakening the popular notion that fast food should be blamed for higher rates of obesity among the poor. (UC Davis study ..., 2011)

In an article in the *New England Journal of Medicine* examining common myths about obesity, the authors state:

> Passionate interests, the human tendency to seek explanations for observed phenomena, and everyday experience appear to contribute to strong convictions about obesity, despite the absence of supporting data. When the public, mass media, government agencies, and even academic scientists espouse unsupported beliefs, the result may be ineffective policy, unhelpful or unsafe clinical and public health recommendations, and an unproductive allocation of resources. (Casazza et al., 2013, p. 446)

Or as Dr. Arya Sharma, founder and Scientific Director of the Canadian Obesity Network, states, "This is not physics, this is physiology!" (Sharma, 2013).

The roots of the complex

Where does this fat complex come from? It is not the result of conscious effort or intent on anyone's part. There is no evidence of a plan to make fat and fat people a target for so much negative attention, bias, and intrusion. Complexes have their roots in the unconscious and this is the case also with the cultural complex—

> As personal complexes emerge out of the level of the personal unconscious in their interaction with deeper levels of the psyche and early parental/familial relationships, cultural complexes can be thought of arising out the cultural unconscious as it interacts with both the archetypal and personal realms of the psyche and the broader outer world arena of schools, communities, media, and all the other forms of cultural and group life. (Singer with Kaplinsky, 2010, p. 4)

The fat complex did not begin with the War on Obesity. In 1961, Richardson and colleagues showed that school children ranked the fat child last on likeability, behind children with various physical handicaps, such as facial disfigurement and using a wheelchair (Richardson, Goodman, Hastorf, & Dornbusch, 1961). And studies showing fat people characterized as lazy, ugly, unhappy, or sloppy date back to the 60s as well. So the bias and negative perceptions are not new.

This heightened focus on obesity as a cultural problem began first in the early 90s, intensified in the middle of that decade and morphed into the War on Obesity after 9/11. This period includes an economic boom, leading to consumption on an ever-larger scale seen in the advent of the so-called "McMansion," a term for over-sized houses on small lots which Word Spy finds first used in print in 1990 (Word Spy, 2015), and the super-sized SUV such as the Hummer. Consumption, luxury, massive size were all taken as benefits of the prosperity brought by the tech boom which fueled much of the economic boom of that period. At the same time, those who could afford consumption on a grand scale, could afford luxury and massive cars and houses, were also expected to be very slender, as if to compensate for the magnitude of consumption. Indeed, clothing size is tied to social class, with an inverse relationship between size and income (Filipovic, 2011). The phrase "Greed is good," taken from the film *Wall Street* became a guiding premise for many. Consumers were urged to consume. After the 9/11 attacks the President asked of Americans: "I ask your continued participation and confidence in the American economy" (The Washington Post, 2001) taken by many to mean they should go out and shop. Greed as one of the Seven Deadly Sins gives rise to guilt. As Callan pointed out, through the scapegoat,

> guilt is ritually returned to the shadowland or the unconscious. It represents everything that has been rejected or repressed by the collective: untempered impulses, greed, aggression, and sexuality ... The community can then return to a blissful and one-sided state of righteousness. (Callan, 2004, p. 4)

The greed of excess consumption gets projected onto fat people, commonly believed to be gluttonous and uncontrolled, and thereby the consumer culture can remain righteous as it spends billions on diet programs and fitness and on food.

A second feature of the period is the rise of international terrorism. With the first World Trade Center bombing, Americans learned that we are not invulnerable to terror attacks. As these attacks continued on US embassies and installations overseas, it began to be apparent that despite the US standing as a superpower, this was an enemy that was far more difficult to defend against. The 9/11 attacks and the bringing down of the World Trade Center drove home the hard reality that we are vulnerable to an enemy we cannot see nor easily ferret out. After so many years of an heroic America ready to save the world for democracy and with a fixed view of ourselves as the bringer of good to the world, these attacks were a great blow and made us anxious about our safety on our own shores for the first time in decades. Terrorism brings dramatically to the forefront our inability to control and protect us from these attacks on our very being. This absence of control, this insecurity, has led, as it often does, to ever more pervasive attempts to control everything possible. As the security measures at airports have proliferated, despite any evidence that they in fact can prevent attacks, so also do attempts to control other things that seem to threaten security and order. Once again, fat people, presumed to be prime examples of lack of discipline and control, became scapegoats for this anxiety about a far more general inability to control our fate.

These factors, greed and anxiety about loss of control, provide fuel from the unconscious for the cultural fat complex. A third force fueling the complex is found when we follow the money. The diet industry, bariatric surgery programs, and pharmaceutical companies all benefit from the panic about weight. The International Obesity Task Force, which was charged by the World Health Organization (WHO) to develop obesity standards, was set up and funded by grants from three pharmaceutical companies, all of which had and have an interest in weight loss drugs (Moynihan, 2006). In 1998 the Task Force declared a change in the definition of overweight and obesity and thus accomplished, by lowering the threshold for determining who is overweight, the movement of at least fifteen million previously normal people into the overweight category overnight. They followed the WHO guidelines and those of another task force at NIH chaired by Xavier Pi-Sunyer, one of the most influential obesity researchers in the country. Pi-Sunyer is tainted by blatant conflicts of interest as he received much of his research support from drug companies with interests in developing obesity drugs and from Weight Watchers where he is a board member (Sourcewatch, F. Xavier Pi-Sunyer, 2015). Conflicts of interest so blatant seemed irrelevant to the selection of Task Force members. The weight loss industry, needless to say, has profited immensely from that decision, a decision that further intensified anxiety about weight and appearance and vastly increased the market for the diet industry.

And there we have it—a culture of greed and ongoing anxiety about loss of control feed increasing focus on obesity as a major issue and the fostering of a cultural fat complex. The complex is heightened and encouraged by the diet and bariatric surgery industries that profit from the concern about disease and cost burdens. And the cultural complex blossoms into the War on Obesity. Which is in fact a war on fat people.

The cultural fat complex permeates every facet of our lives from mass media to fashion to accepted standards for beauty and attraction, to what we can and cannot eat, to healthcare and employment. Two-thirds of American women wear a size fourteen or above (Meltzer, 2015). This means there is a large market to be served, yet most women's clothing stores do not carry apparel above a size eighteen. Those mainstream clothing retailers like Old Navy or J Jill that do offer larger sizes do not in their retail stores; to purchase their "plus size" or "women's size" items, a customer must shop online or from a catalog. From a *New Yorker* article on plus-size fashion:

> … I heard people making reference to the fashion industry's "closet" plus-size designers: accessible luxury brands with big licensing businesses—including Calvin Klein, Vince Camuto, Ralph Lauren, Tommy Hilfiger, and Michael Kors. All have plus-size lines that are sold in stores like Macy's but are not advertised.
>
> Some people in the plus-size fashion world have attempted to persuade them to be more vocal, to little avail … Nicolette Mason, a columnist for *Marie Claire* and a blogger, said that she had made it a mission to persuade Michael Kors to acknowledge his "beautiful" plus-size line, Michael. "I tried to get samples from Michael Kors, and they wouldn't lend them to me," she said. "They pretty much said that they would not publicize their plus brand." When I contacted Michael Kors, a public-relations representative sent over a statement: "The Michael Kors plus size line launched in 2007. Michael prides himself on being able to dress women of all shapes and sizes, and making them feel and look good." (Widdecombe, 2014)

In the fashion industry, letting it be known by advertising or publicizing openly that a designer known for high fashion also has a plus-size line is considered damaging to the brand. To be known to want the business of fat women, they believe, damages the brand image.

The fat body is seen as ugly, unhealthy, immoral, undisciplined, out of control, sexless, a failed body. And therefore rightfully subject to this war against fat, because it represents a scourge that must be eliminated.

CHAPTER THREE

When a body meets a body:
fat enters the consulting room

Over the course of my lifetime I have seen five therapists for more than a session or two. Each time, without fail, I have encountered what I call the thin gaze and with it the assumption that I should want to lose weight. The thin gaze, arising from thin privilege, is the objectifying gaze cast upon the fat person by someone who is not fat. One therapist, a man who himself was fat, assumed that I should want to lose weight because otherwise how could I ever feel desirable? Each time, with all of them, I was angry, though that anger remained unexpressed. Inside, under the anger, I felt shame and pain. Why was what concerned me of so little interest or value? Why was anything I was concerned about automatically filtered through the therapist's notions about my weight, even when weight was not the object of my concern, at least not then? How was it that when they saw me, they saw my weight more than they saw me, a woman with her own concerns and issues?

After my second child was born, I was quite depressed. I had spent three and a half months on bed rest during the pregnancy. Both my life and my child's were at risk. When he was born, I terminated my fertility because to risk another pregnancy was to seriously jeopardize my life. And within a month of his birth, I learned of my husband's infidelity during my pregnancy. All during the time I was confined to bed rest, I told myself I could fall apart after he was born. But instead of falling apart I felt crushed by depression, able to do little else than care for my baby and his three-year-old sister. So I decided to see a therapist, a woman who had five children and was said to be particularly sensitive to issues of mothering and marriage. I took my baby with me when I saw her. I told her all about what had happened. I felt I was dying inside. I needed to be heard and cared for, helped to find my way back to myself and to being alive. I was dying inside and what did she want to focus on? My weight. Again and again, I told her weight was not on my agenda, that I needed to sort out my life on a far more basic level. But she persisted. Frustrated that she simply wouldn't/couldn't hear me, I terminated with her. She sent me off with a dire statement that if I didn't deal with my weight now, I would regret it. Despite the fact that I was clearly depressed, hanging on by my fingernails, all she saw was that I was fat and she believed that I had to "deal with" my weight, meaning I should lose weight, in order to heal. Indeed for her, that I was not interested in focusing on my weight meant I was in denial and that I would suffer the consequences. Did she ever even hear me, I wonder, when I struggled to talk about my sadness about no longer being able to have children, about not feeling as alive to my new baby as I wanted to be, about my slowly failing marriage or did she only see my fat body?

When I turned forty, I had two children and an unhappy marriage. Intrigued with Jungian psychology, I had been reading everything I could find and attended workshops and seminars presented by Jungians of one kind and another. I began to think about maybe becoming a Jungian analyst, which meant finding an analyst and entering a Jungian analysis. Around that time a woman analyst, fresh from Zurich, moved to Maine and I began to see her. I needed to accumulate hours in analysis in order to apply for training, yes, but more than that I was forty and I knew I needed to deal with what I wanted in my life, things that had eluded me up to then. She was the kind of woman, slender and well dressed, who made me feel clumsy and ungainly. Even the chairs in her consulting room seemed meant for someone small and dainty. To top it all off, she looked very much like my mother. When we started, maybe even in the first session, I said something to her to the effect that the issue of my weight was non-negotiable. In my thirties I had worked too long and hard making an uneasy peace with my body, by stopping dieting and hating myself for being fat, to be willing to step into the madness of dieting again. In spite of that declaration or maybe because of it, early on she told me a dream she had when she was in analysis. At the time her own analyst was fat and she believed she had the dream for her. In her dream, Jung told her "every extra ounce costs a pound of consciousness." Her analyst had been grateful to her for telling her the dream, she said. I was not grateful. Not at all. I was furious that despite what I had stated as my concerns, she ignored me. I did not directly voice my anger to her, though I did write to her about it. I wrote to her about it because I had not yet found my voice to express my anger and my truth. I wanted her to hear me, see me as I was, and allow me to open up to her, and to myself, about my experience in my body, in my life. I needed to speak and be heard, all of me, without the blame I felt so often that all I had to do to be "normal" was to eat less and move more. I wanted her to see more than my weight. But that was not to be.

As is common among Jungians, she saw a fairy tale as a means to approach again the subject of weight. She wanted me to work with her using an English fairy tale, "The Laidly Worm of Spindleston Heugh" (The Laidly Worm of Spindleston Heugh, n.d.), a tale she connected to hunger and the mother complex. I read it. But the armor of anger I had already put on against her kept me from engaging the story with her. I did not trust her enough to make myself vulnerable to the degree necessary to explore with her the issues of my body, hunger, my mother, and my weight. Undaunted she asked if I would consider losing at least a few pounds. Had she heard nothing of what I had told her? Could she not see or accept that I was not willing to deal with this issue with her? I was furious. How many pounds would be enough? Ten? Twenty? Fifty? What would be enough? What made it acceptable for her to impose that desire on me? Why should I step again into that madness just to satisfy her? She had no answer. We never spoke about it again in the three years I worked with her. And I am sorry to say I never dealt directly with how I felt about her and about that whole episode.

Like most fat people, I have had a long line of people in my life all too eager to police my body by shaming, cajoling or trying to make me cede control of my eating to someone or something, anything but my own desires. When she told me her dream, she said to me, as Jung said in the dream, that every extra ounce of weight cost me a pound of consciousness. Whether she intended it or not, for me she was saying that in and of itself, my body was pathological and by extension, because she was slender, she was superior to me. I felt anything of my own experience and feelings about my life, my body, my desires was less important to her than were I to take on the effort to lose weight as a demonstration of something—co-operation perhaps or desire to heal. Her countertransference, fully in synch with the cultural complex, met my internalized loathing of my body and fat, also lodged in that complex, and served to push me away from her. My negative mother complex was activated with a vengeance. I was again that little girl who defied her mother. I believed I could not risk opening up what it is like to be fat, to fully experience the thin gaze, to feel the judgment and disgust that is part of the everyday life of fat people. And I hadn't the courage to confront her. She seemed unable to fully appreciate and relate to what Susan Gutwill understands: "fatness is also seen as reason to blame the fat person who ate his or her way into 'freakishness'" (Gutwill, 1994b, p. 154). Gutwill continues, writing of a patient of hers:

> She [her patient] needed to hear her experience of herself articulated. She needed to hear the actual word: "freak." she needed for her therapist to validate that, in her fat body, Rebecca was truly and objectively the target of people's worst fears, projections and hatred. Rebecca needed the reality testing that such mirroring of her own buried knowledge articulated. Once articulated, she could see her experience and begin to grieve for it and also begin to trust other parts of her inner knowledge, including how lovely, loving, and competent she was. As with any survivor of trauma, Rebecca needs to own the truth of her past order to move on from it. (Gutwill, 1994b, p. 159)

I needed support and understanding to be able to look at my own freakishness, a state I already and always felt, so that like Gutwill's patient, I could digest the truth of my own body and life. But she could not do that. Thus one of the most important issues in my life never was addressed with her because she could not put herself in my shoes and listen to my experience. She was not a bad analyst. My need brought her up against her limitations and made us a bad fit with each other.

I have been thinking and writing about the essay, "Fat Lady" in Irvin Yalom's book, *Love's Executioner*, which I read soon after it was published in 1989, for years. I began working with a male analyst not long after reading Yalom's book. I was greatly troubled by that essay. It made me angry and at the same time fearful that my analyst saw me the way Yalom saw Betty. I was horrified by what he wrote:

> The day Betty entered my office, the instant I saw her steering her ponderous two-hundred-fifty-pound, five-foot-two-inch frame toward my trim, high-tech office chair, I knew that a great trial of countertransference was in store for me.
>
> I have always been repelled by fat women. I find them disgusting: their absurd sidewise waddle, their absence of body contour, breasts, laps, buttocks, shoulders, jawlines, cheekbones, everything, everything I like to see in a woman, obscured in an avalanche of flesh. And I hate their clothes, the shapeless, baggy dresses or, worse, the stiff elephantine blue jeans with the barrel thighs. How dare they impose that body on the rest of us? (Yalom, 1989, pp. 94–95)

In those days I worried that my analyst was feeling the same disgust Yalom felt as he sat across from me. I felt self-conscious before entering the room where we met. I remember photocopying the essay and giving it to him to read. I wanted him to find Yalom's attitude awful. I wanted him to understand that I feared he felt like that toward me and to reassure me but when I tried to articulate that desire, the words would not come. Because I was in the grip of the thin gaze, what he felt hardly mattered because I had interiorized it to the point that I was my own overseer, just as Foucault said of the prisoner in the panopticon.

Yalom has been much praised for openly admitting such strong prejudice, such clear negative countertransference. And indeed it takes some courage to openly admit such feelings. But in most of what I have read about that essay, no one questions that his revulsion in fact dominates the entire therapy. Nor are questions raised that he could think and feel this: "How dare they impose that body on the rest of us?" as if any of his patients owe it to him to be pleasing to his eye. Then again, it is acceptable to hate fat and to think ill of fat people so there was little chance of serious criticism except from the fat acceptance community whose opinions could be dismissed as defensive. Nevertheless, he does deserve credit for daring to say what no doubt many therapists think. And what I feared my own analyst felt.

In the course of the treatment described in Yalom's essay, Betty loses 100 pounds. Of course, because weight is seen as the cause of her depression, because she loses so much weight, the therapy is deemed spectacularly successful. Another story is revealed in the end of the essay when Yalom says:

> "It's the same with me, Betty. I'll miss our meetings. But I'm changed as a result of knowing you."
>
> She had been crying, her eyes downcast, but at my words she stopped sobbing and looked toward me, expectantly.
>
> "And, even though we won't meet again, I'll still retain that change."
>
> "What change?"
>
> "Well, as I mentioned to you, I hadn't had much professional experience with the problem of obesity." I noted Betty's eyes drop with disappointment and silently berated myself for being so impersonal.
>
> "Well, what I mean is that I hadn't worked before with heavy patients, and I've gotten a new appreciation for the problems of ..." I could see from her expression that she was sinking even deeper into disappointment. "What I mean is that my attitude about obesity has changed a lot. When we started I personally didn't feel comfortable with obese people."
>
> In unusually feisty terms, Betty interrupted me. "Ho! ho! ho! Didn't feel comfortable. That's putting it mildly. Do you know that for the first six months you hardly ever looked at me? And in a whole year and a half you've never, not once, touched me? Not even for a handshake!"
>
> My heart sank. My God, she's right! I have never touched her. I simply hadn't realized it. And I guess I didn't look at her very often either. I hadn't expected her to notice! (Yalom, 1989, p. 123)

Yalom was naïve to think that his distaste for Betty's body had not been evident to her. She lived in a world that reviled her body and likely she, like me, expected to encounter judgment. A more interesting question is why, given that she knew all along of his distaste, did she continue to work with him? The answer? She herself carries and directs those same feelings of disgust at herself.

We don't know how Betty is now, more than nearly thirty years later. Statistically she most likely has regained all of the weight lost and probably gained more. That is what happens when we try to tame the body through dieting. She may have had bariatric surgery and be among the minority who have not experienced complications from the surgery. Or perhaps she is in that tiny minority who succeeded in maintaining that weight loss. But in the years since the essay was published, no one questioned what losing weight was about for her and how working with a therapist filled with contempt and disgust for her body affected her feelings about herself. If even the therapist finds one's body repulsive, given that the repulsion is not expressed.

It is all but impossible for a fat person, no matter the reasons for being fat, not to have a host of emotional issues about her size and her body. Every day the culture is telling her that she is too big, too much, not acceptable. Finding the courage to talk about those feelings in the presence of someone who finds her as disgusting as she herself often does is quite a feat. How does she find her voice about her anger at what she encounters? How is she to lovingly care about her body and for herself if her therapist sees her body with the contempt and hatred she herself so often feels? And what if she is tired of having to devote herself to losing all that weight? The operative assumption is that in a room with a normal weight therapist and a fat patient, it is the patient who has a weight problem. What is it at work that makes it so difficult for the fat patient to be perceived as a whole person who might not share much less welcome the therapist's agenda about her weight? As Susan Gutwill puts it: "The burden of an unrelenting hatred of one's body is an experience that must be acknowledged and brought into the therapy room on its own terms" (Gutwill, 1994b, p. 160).

The consulting room does not offer protection from cultural complexes much as we might wish it did. Both patient and therapist come together shaped and influenced by them. Kimbles points out:

> ... it should be obvious that the unconscious idioms, identifications, affect structures that contribute to a sense of being a person within a particular reference group will also become active contributors to transference and countertransference and at times make the interpretation of these dynamics difficult. Cultural differences may complicate the treatment process by generating guilt, aggression, and denial about the role of differences, and the conflict of complexes that results can generate excessive ambivalence, curiosity, doubt, defensiveness, and confusion. (Kimbles, 2004, p. 202)

One consequence of the dominance of the fat cultural complex is that it affects how fat people are treated even in settings where care and concern should be expectable. However, study after study has shown that members of the healing professions are also in the grip of this complex and attribute the responsibility for fat to the fat person. The Rudd Center located at the University of Connecticut has done extensive work exploring weight stigma and bias among healthcare professionals. Their report documents findings of a number of large surveys. Saguy summarizes this data:

> A survey of 89 general practitioners (GPs) with medical practices throughout the United Kingdom showed that, on average, GPs considered their patients' tendency to eat too much, to eat the wrong foods, or not to get enough exercise as greater contributors to their obesity than genetics, glandular/hormonal factors, or metabolism. Another study ... arrived at a similar conclusion, finding that providers believed that physical inactivity, overeating, food addiction, and personality characteristics were the most important causes of overweight. A study of 600 general practitioners in France found that 30 percent considered overweight and obese patients to be lazier and more self-indulgent than normal-weight people, and 60 percent considered lack of motivation to be the most common problem in treating overweight and obesity. In another study of 620 primary care physicians in the United States, more than 50 percent reported viewing obese patients as awkward, unattractive, ugly, or noncompliant. One-third of the sample further characterized these patients as weak-willed, sloppy, and lazy. (Saguy, 2012, p. 74)

In June of 2014, at the annual meeting of the American Association of Nurse Practitioners a study of bias among nurse practitioners against obese patients reported:

> ... more than 50% of the clinicians surveyed agreed with statements that:
>
> Overweight people are not as good as others.
> Overweight people are not as successful as others.
> Overweight people are tidy.
> Overweight people are not as healthy as others.
> Most people do not wish to marry an overweight person.

Overweight people have family issues.
Overweight is the result of overeating.
Overweight people are addicted to food. (Susman, 2014)

Psychotherapists of all persuasions, though they couch their bias in different terms, also lay the responsibility for fat at the feet of the fat patient, generally seeing it a consequence of overeating and/or compulsive eating in service of one or another underlying emotional issue. The Rudd Center reports: "Psychologists ascribe more pathology, more negative and severe symptoms, and worse prognosis to obese patients compared to thinner patients presenting identical psychological profiles" (Rudd Brief, 2009).

Even when well intended, this tendency to ascribe pathology to fat people seeps in. Kathy Leach, a practitioner of Transactional Analysis (TA) in the UK, looks at treating fat people in her book, *The Overweight Patient: A Psychological Approach to Understanding and Working with Obesity*. She opens with acknowledging that if losing weight were easy, fat people would do so. But she then moves into her theory that people who are fat become so as a way of armoring themselves, of protecting themselves and concludes that their weight is a survival decision. From her promising opening, she goes into the usual assumption that fat people are responsible for being fat and that therapy can, through the process of discovering the reasons, lead them to becoming normal. Leach effectively says if only the fat person would straighten out her thinking, life would change and she would no longer be fat:

> I am working to find out *why the patient needs to maintain a large size or to eat excessively* ... My goal is for the patient to have a choice about her weight loss and that genuine psychological and social choice comes from knowing why she has needed to overeat or be big in the world in order to cope. (Leach, 2009, p. 14) [Emphasis added]

Once again we see the cultural complex at play.

A problem with nearly all of what has been written about psychotherapeutic approaches to dealing with fat is the underlying basic assumption that fat is an indicator of pathology and that psychotherapeutically treating whatever the underlying emotional/psychological issues will result in weight loss and achievement of a normal weight.

There seems to be no awareness of the complexity of obesity or of the dismal success rate in achieving and maintaining long-term weight loss, regardless of the method employed. The therapeutic imagination for the most part seems to be unable to conceptualize fat as anything other than pathological. In an article looking at sexual satisfaction of obese women, the author does an excellent review of the psychotherapeutic literature on obesity and notes an important study in which Stunkard (1996) concludes:

> When psychopathology is observed in obese individuals, it is now seen as a consequence rather than a cause—a consequence of the prejudice and discrimination to which the overweight are subjected. (Stunkard, 1996, p. 163)

I consider myself a Jungian. Though I wish it were otherwise, I have seen no evidence that Jungians are free of the cultural fat complex. Nonetheless I am puzzled by the silence in the Jungian literature about obesity, an issue that preoccupies so much of the culture. In fact in my research, to my surprise I discovered little in that literature about body at all and most especially about the female body. In the analytic encounter, body meets body, yet rarely is body spoken of.

Anorexia warrants books and articles, but on obesity, nothing. We find mention often of the need to connect with the body, of the body as a storehouse of memory. *Quadrant*, a major Jungian journal, on their website describes itself as a journal of "essays grounded in personal and professional experience, which focus on issues of matter and body, psyche and spirit." But in the archives of *Quadrant* I find nothing about fat, save for one article in 2009, "The epidemic of obesity in contemporary american culture: A jungian reflection" (Darlington, 2009) which focuses on compulsive eating. As is so often the case and consistent with the dominant narrative of the cultural complex, fat is equated with gluttony. Marion Woodman's book, *The Owl Was A Baker's Daughter* is the only book in all of the Jungian literature to deal with obesity. In the *Journal of Analytical Psychology*, with archives spanning over sixty years, there are but eight articles that even contain the word obesity and none that considers obesity as itself and what it means. In what was the *San Francisco Library Journal* now *Jung Journal: Culture & Psyche*, there are two interviews with Marion Woodman, in which some of her thoughts about fat are offered within reviews of her two books which dealt with fat and anorexia. And that is it, all that I have been able to find on the subject in the Jungian literature. The culture at large is preoccupied with obesity and the war it has declared on obesity, but the Jungian world, judging by its literature, is blind to it. As Jung wrote:

> We do not like to look at the shadow-side of ourselves; therefore there are many people in civilized society who have lost there shadow altogether, have lost the third dimension, and with it they have usually lost the body. The body is a most doubtful friend because it produces things we do not like: there are too many things about the personification of this shadow of the ego. Sometimes it forms the skeleton in the cupboard, and everybody naturally wants to get rid of such a thing. (Jung, 1976b, p. 23)

Is the assumption that fat is a symptom of underlying conflict and complexes so deep, so axiomatic that it warrants no challenge? Is it that fat disgusts us, as we saw in Yalom with his patient Betty? Barry Miller's thoughts are about homosexuality but can well be applied to fat and obesity as well:

> It is useful to reflect upon how disgust is dealt with in an analytic situation … Does the analyst relate to disgust as something to be overcome or something to penetrate more deeply? Can the analyst tolerate disgust about a racial type, a form of sexual expression, unwanted desires, or even certain ideas? Is the analytic work inclined toward the dissolution of this disgust or the pursuit of its use in the life of an individual? … The possibility here is that a contemporary psychotherapist might react to the disgust … by seeing it as something to be overcome rather than finding its relevance or purpose to his life. It is at these intersections that the analyst is challenged to separate his or her own values and goals from the process of the other individual, the analysand, who has another agenda for these feelings and attitudes. (B. Miller, 2010, p. 116)

"Can the analyst tolerate disgust about a racial type, a form of sexual expression, unwanted desires, or even certain ideas?" Miller asks. Yalom's disgust and its role in his work with Betty are apparent from his statements about how he saw her when she came to him. I do not believe it is a stretch to assume that disgust about fat and believing fat bodies are repulsive underlies much of various psychotherapeutic approaches to fat patients. Because of this, when dealing with fat patients, it seems more than usually important for the therapist to be aware of her own biases, attitudes, and complexes around weight and appearance. In an article about countertransference with an obese patient, Drell noted:

> In examining one's countertransference responses to obese patients in psychotherapy, it is important to note that the obese patient's appearance may actually be repulsive, distorting the human physique to grotesque proportions … Therapists should intermittently ask themselves how they feel about their patients' obesity and how they have minimized or exaggerated the meaning of the patients' excess weight. If in the course of therapy, the patients' obesity is to discussed or if it is discussed to the exclusion of other issues, therapists should examine their countertransference responses as well as the patients' resistances. (Drell, 1988, p. 79)

Note the language he uses, words like "repulsive" and "grotesque," with which he betrays his feeling that of course such bodies arouse disgust. Even in recognizing countertransference, Drell's own feelings about fat bodies appear to be leaking out.

A few years ago a woman in analytic training in Zurich contacted me. She was doing her thesis on knitting and had heard that I am both a knitter and a Jungian and hoped I might be able to point her to some sources she had overlooked. After she completed her training, she again contacted me about the possibility of our meeting. She sent her thesis to me by way of thanks for some suggestions I had made and from it, I learned of her own history with eating disorders. We met for coffee one summer Sunday. The meeting went fairly well in spite of the occasional difference of opinion. Then she asked me about my current interests. I started talking about my writing and thinking about fat and the Jungian world. As I talked about the data on the overall failure of diets, things took a turn. She asserted that if only I would do what she had done by joining Food Addicts Anonymous and following their program, I would lose weight, keep it off and be healthy. As I often do in situations where I am angry and don't feel free to express my anger, I responded intellectually, citing research which supported my position. When I asked if she believed that she should urge weight loss for any fat patient who came to see her, she said yes because she would want them to be "healthy." At that point I tried to politely back us out of the whole topic. Time to part and we said our polite farewells.

I responded to her assertion intellectually. I wished later I had let her know at the time about my emotional response. Unsolicited advice is seldom welcomed by anyone. It is a sad fact that people feel free to offer advice to fat people because the belief is widespread that we are responsible for our weight and somehow it is a matter of ignorance that we have failed to take our ample selves in hand and discipline mind and body so as to become "normal" weight. But more than that, she betrayed a deeply held conviction that her agenda about weight is the correct agenda when it comes to dealing with a fat patient, that her belief that the only way for such a patient to be healthy is to lose weight, and that losing weight is a worthy and important goal in therapy no matter what the patient wants or believes. And that it is acceptable, even desirable to tell fat people what they should do to lose weight under the cover of concern for their health.

For that analyst, as for Yalom, and most therapists, it is a given that my fat is something that must be gotten rid of. As anthropologist Gayle Rubin has noted of homosexuality, "The search for a cause is a search for something that could change so that these 'problematic' [phenomena] would simply not occur." In other words, discussions about what causes homosexuality or obesity are driven by the assumption that it would be better if these phenomena did not exist at all (Saguy, 2012, p. 70).

From there it is not a big leap to the assumption that it would be better were there no fat people at all, if we did not exist. Alarmist? Yes, but not as great a leap as it might seem. All of the cultural notions about fat—the disgust, the belief that it represents unbridled appetite and all of the other common cultural beliefs—are part of the background of belief, unexamined and unconscious for most therapists and others in helping professions, gripped as they and most of our culture are by the fat complex. Stripped to basics, the belief is that the world would be a better place without fat, and hence fat people, therefore fat and fat people must be battled as an enemy. There is hope, as Kimbles suggests:

> With an openness to the likely presence of cultural complexes, whether in competition or collusion, however, the opportunities for both patient and analyst to see what the unconscious has been doing with the fact of differences and to observe how this gets represented and narrated in the unfolding analysis, is rich indeed. (Kimbles, 2004, p. 202)

Philosopher A. O. Lovejoy described the human propensity that leads to the kind of climate in which we now live:

> It is the beliefs which are so much a matter of course that they are rather tacitly presupposed than formally expressed and argued for, the ways of thinking which seem so natural and inevitable that they are not scrutinized with the eye of logical self-consciousness, that often are the most decisive of the character of a philosopher's doctrine, and still oftener of the dominant intellectual tendencies of an age. (Lovejoy, 1976, p. 7)

McLuhan more succinctly says, "I don't know who discovered water, but I know it wasn't the fish" (Quote investigator, n.d.). We all swim in a toxic mix of fear, disgust, judgment, and hatred of fat, leading us to see fat by itself as evil in the world, of something to be eradicated like a dreaded disease. The fat person becomes responsible for this cursed state. The complex, as we have seen earlier, is so pervasive and powerful that it seems natural and normal, unquestionable.

Thanks to the powers of the media and the power of the cultural complex, it is fair to say that most therapists, along with the people we encounter everywhere every day, assume that fat people are gluttons who eat huge portions of "unhealthy" foods like piles of doughnuts, mammoth plates of pasta, a whole pizza, junk foods of all kinds. Google "fat people eating" and the popular images show this. After all, how else could they have become fat, if not from gorging themselves on junk foods of all kinds? It is almost impossible for most people to imagine a fat person eating a salad or other foods considered "healthy." And almost as difficult to imagine a slender person devouring excessive amounts of junk foods. If we stop to think about it, we realize that of course, fat people eat salads and slender people gorge themselves sometimes. It is simply not possible to determine how or what a person eats by looking at her. Thin privilege leads people to assume that the way they eat is what allows them to be thin and that if fat people ate that same way, they too would be thin. As Gutwill notes

> Therapists are easily or subtly prey to the cultural mandates for the female body ... This mandate is ... fat phobic, obsessed with bodily control, in revolt against aging and its concomitant bodily changes,

outraged at and contemptuous of the imperfect out-of-control body and repulsed by immodest female appetites and hunger. (Gutwill, 1994, p. 154)

The assumption that it is compulsive eating which lies at the heart of obesity is one of those beliefs that Lovejoy described as so much a part of common "knowledge" that it goes unquestioned. This assumption is a significant part of Marion Woodman's theory about obesity, which I will discuss later. The only other Jungian I can find who has written about it, Beth Darlington, entirely conflates fat and gluttony and compulsive eating (Darlington, 2009). Yet all of her sources for her information about obesity come from articles in the press, with no reference to even mainstream research which counters the dominant narrative about fat. The journal *Quadrant* gives the following as keywords for her article: obesity, gorging, overeating, gluttony, hunger.

In her most recent book, *The Mystery of Analytical Work*, Barbara Stevens Sullivan brings together Jung and Bion. In my own practice I have tried for many years to hew to Bion's dictum to approach each patient, each hour without memory, desire or understanding. Sullivan does a lovely job of explicating what this means in practice. Of the three, I find eschewing desire to be especially important. This means setting aside any agenda for the patient, any wish that I have about the patient. To quote her:

A desire to help the patient is similar: is the patient inducing in me a subjective sense of helplessness or weakness? Is he bringing up a savior complex or sadistically rubbing my nose in the "helplessness" I feel when faced with his "extraordinary" pain? In wanting to help, am I unconsciously striving to exclude some level of suffering that is trying to enter the room? The desire to help the patient will mean something slightly different every time it comes up, even with the same patient, let alone with different people. But whatever its precipitant, the desire blinds the analyst to the ways the patient needs to be seen and accepted in his wounded condition, as is, before he can begin to let it go. This desire to help is a particularly seductive one. Our patients want us to help them and most therapists entered the field out of a conscious wish to help people. But it is important to let go of the wish because, as far as we can tell, it is usually not helpful to try to help. Trying to understand the patient as he is generally loosens his character structure and begins or reinforces a

> growth process inside him that leads to positive ("helpful") devel-
> opments in his inner world. (Stevens Sullivan, 2009, p. 217)

Darlington and Woodman, my first analyst, and my coffee companion of that summer Sunday all fall prey to the same bias against fat that we see in other health professionals and like most therapists, are unable to set aside their own agenda about weight and the judgments about weight from the culture and simply listen to the patient and her experience. As Sullivan said, "the desire [to help] blinds the analyst to the ways the patient needs to be seen and accepted in his wounded condition, as is, before he can begin to let it go" and sometimes even in letting it go, the resulting change is not what the therapist might wish, that is, that the patient lose weight.

Reparative therapy or, as it is also known, conversion therapy, is psychotherapeutic treatment aiming to convert homosexual and transgender people into heterosexuals, the assumption being that heterosexuality is what is normal and healthy. It capitalizes on those members of the LGBT community who are conflicted and/or self-loathing about their sexual orientation and identity and promises to make them happy and normal provided that they renounce homosexuality. In essence, as in the obesity narrative, the sufferer is blamed for his or her suffering. The failure rate of these therapies is nearly 100 percent over time.

As the fog of a cultural complex about homosexuality has slowly been clearing, we have seen within recent decades the removal of sexual orientation from the *Diagnostic and Statistical Manual* as a psychiatric disorder and the rise of condemnation of these conversion therapies as unethical with increasing pressure to make them illegal as well. This represents a major change from seeing homosexuality as pathological and something to be "cured."

How different is reparative therapy really from the multitude of failed therapeutic approaches to treating obesity? The underlying assumptions are the same—both homosexuals and fat people are seen as responsible for their own suffering, as pathological, disgusting, and a departure from what nature (or God) intends. Both assume an absence of self-discipline, inability to curb appetite, and lack of moral strength. Both treatments have a near total failure rate. And in neither approach is serious attention given to the misery that can come from being a member of a marginalized and judged community. The essential message in both is "Repent your evil ways and you will be saved from your life of sin and misery."

The dominant paradigm in psychotherapy research favors cognitive behavioral approaches because of the belief that it is more scientifically based and standardized and therefore is more amenable to short-term outcome studies. Therefore there is little to no funding for any other approaches. It should come as no surprise then that when a psychological component is included in obesity treatment, it is invariably behavioral. Weight Watchers has included these principles since the early 90s drawing on research by psychologist Kelly Brownell.

In 2012:

> the U.S. Preventive Services Task Force urged doctors to identify patients with a body mass index (BMI) of 30 or more and either provide counseling themselves or refer the patient to a program designed to promote weight loss and improve health prospects ... These programs would set weight-loss goals, improve knowledge about nutrition, teach patients how to track their eating and set limits, identify barriers to change (such as a scarcity of healthful food choices near home) and strategise on ways to maintain life-style changes. (Healy, 2012)

Anticipating that psychologists could play a large role in the mandate for treatment and treatment guidelines under the Affordable Care Act, the American Psychological Association convened a panel to develop guidelines to address the problem of obesity:

> ... for much of the population, obesity is associated with disease and mortality. It can be effectively treated through behavior change, which falls within the domain of psychologists. As collaborations between psychologists and other healthcare professionals increase, psychologists are expected to be called upon more frequently to address obesity and other physical conditions. (APA to establish treatment guideline panels, 2012)

Linda Bacon writes:

> The [Affordable Care] Act enforces the recent recommendation from the U.S. Preventive Services Task Force stating that all doctors should warn "obese" patients that their weight puts them at high risk for disease, but that weight loss and lifestyle changes can help—and

then direct them to intensive weight-loss counseling. Currently, few insurance companies pay for such programs. Under "Obamacare," however, insurers will be required to cover most medically advised weight-loss expenses and employers will almost surely intensify their anti-obesity campaigns. Weight Watchers' stock has already surged in anticipation of the bounty to come. (Bacon, 2012)

But notice that no consideration is given to consulting or including fat people. Again we see thin privilege at work, in the way that notes:

I have benefited from thin privilege ... in that people tend to attribute positive traits to me and other thin people solely because of our body weight. Because of my relative thinness, I am often unfairly considered a more objective, and thus more credible, commentator on debates over fatness than if I were fat ... In this sense, thinness in our culture is what sociologists call an "unmarked category." (Saguy, 2012, p. 25)

Evidence does not exist that obesity can be effectively treated over the long term through behavioral change. No so-called treatment for obesity has a more than five to ten percent success rate long term. Most types of cancer have better prognoses. And how is it ethical to promote a treatment that fails almost every time within five years, thereby increasing the suffering and shame that brings most fat people to seek change in the first place? The APA panel issued a briefing sheet in 2014 "to help psychologists solve the obesity epidemic in the U.S. ... offering direction on how to prevent obesity and treat the one-third of Americans with the disease" (American Psychological Association, 2014). Again there is no input from fat people nor were any fat people included on the panel that issued the briefing sheet. Nor are there any approaches suggested for dealing with fat stigma. There is no recognition of the absence of any evidence for any weight loss method with more than a very slight long-term success rate. What the APA proposes as the ways psychologists can help is:

- Psychologists play an integral role in the treatment of obesity by providing effective interventions that include self-monitoring of eating habits and physical activity, stress management, stimulus control, contingency management, cognitive restructuring, and social support.

- Psychologists can also assist primary care physicians in tracking patient behaviors related to diet, physical activity, and weight; providing more consistent guidance for patients; improving time efficiency during visits; and promoting integrated care. Fewer than half of primary care physicians reported providing specific guidance on diet, physical activity, or weight control, and fewer than 22% reported routinely and systematically monitoring patients' behaviors or other measures of progress related to diet, physical activity, or weight.
- Weight-loss surgery is an additional option for weight reduction in a limited number of patients meeting criteria for clinically severe obesity (i.e., body mass index >40 or >35 kg/m^2 with comorbid conditions).
- Psychological evaluations to determine emotional stability/readiness for surgery are not only critical for patient safety and success but are also now required by insurance companies.
- Psychoeducational groups and support groups, as well as individual counseling, have been used as effective supplemental treatment approaches for weight-loss surgery.
- Many studies have supported the effectiveness of behavioral therapy, cognitive-behavioral therapy, mindfulness, and motivational interviewing interventions for weight loss in obese patients.
- Psychologists have the knowledge and training to assist with the prevention of weight problems, adherence to weight-loss programs, and maintenance of healthy weight and lifestyle, which are greatly needed to address the current obesity epidemic. *The American Psychological Association is currently developing clinical practice guidelines for the treatment of obesity based on systematic reviews of the scientific literature.* (Briefing series on the role of psychology in health care: Adult obesity, 2014) [Emphasis added]

Notice the concluding statement. If this were true, then that review would include the extensive literature on stigma, anti-fat bias, and the fallacy of there being anything like a simple behavioral solution to something as complex in origin as obesity. In fact more evidence of the harm arising from anti-fat bias appeared very recently. In their study, Sutin and colleagues conclude:

The association between mortality and weight discrimination was generally stronger than that between mortality and other attributions for discrimination. In addition to its association with poor health outcomes, weight discrimination may shorten life expectancy. (Sutin, Stephan, & Terracciano, 2015, p. 1803)

I am not holding my breath. As one of the respected critics of psychiatric over-reach, the psychiatrist who writes the blog 1 Boring Old Man says:

> Therapeutic Zeal. It's the danger behind the Hippocratic Oath's injunction to "Do No Harm." These radical treatments were introduced for the devastating, often fatal illnesses only seen behind the walls of Asylums and State Hospitals. But with some successes, they were increasingly applied in patients with less debilitating illness or diagnoses. That's what Therapeutic Zeal means, becoming too invested in treating and overlooking the dangers. (1 Boring Old Man, 2013)

These interventions are proposed in the guise of helping fat people to become "normal," acceptable, slender. And they carry at least the hint of coercion with penalties such as increased premiums for health insurance if the fat person does not comply.

There is very little written about body meeting body in psychotherapy of any kind. When patient and therapist sit down together, they are meeting body-to-body as well as mind-to-mind. And each brings with her all of her assumptions, feelings, and projections about bodies, both her own and that of the other. Jane Burka, in an unusual example of a fat therapist writing about her experience, writes:

> … heavy people represent a threat because they embody a pervasive fear that underlies our culture: the loss of self-control. Heavy women are considered lazy and self-indulgent, lacking self-regulation. They have given into their impulses instead of restricting them. They have not harnessed themselves to moderation. We live in an era in which greed is supposed to be expressed through ambition, not indulgence; in which we are led toward excessive consumption of products and services, not food. The standards for what is or is not attractive become equated with what is good or bad, right or wrong, and so matters of appearance become confused with issues of morality. (Burka, 2001, p. 258)

This is as true for the fat therapist as for the slender one.

In the years that we have worked together, my analyst and I have both learned about the toxic waters of the cultural fat complex. Many years ago he asked my permission to use a dream of mine in a paper he was writing. I agreed. He gave me the finished paper to read and asked how I felt about it. In reading it, I discovered a phrase he used in his description of me, a phrase that infuriated me, "her weight belies her intelligence." I wanted him to remove it but it had gone to press already. I was angry and afraid that what I had feared was true, that he in fact believed that my weight and my intelligence were mutually exclusive somehow.

We talked and argued about that phrase many times over the years, each time broadening our understanding of what it meant, both to me and to him. I became better able to say what was false about it, about the bias inherent in it. I became clearer about what it was that upset me and how to express that and how it fit into my history of living in a non-conforming body. And he came to see it was in fact a ridiculous thing to say and tell me that he would not use it were he writing now.

When he wrote it, in the grip of the cultural fat complex with its attendant thin privilege, what he said seemed reasonable. Of course one would expect fat is a marker for lack of intelligence, because after all if a person is intelligent, she would control her weight. And of course because I had internalized all of the negative messages of the complex, instead of expressing my anger, I felt shame and disappointment. Thin privilege creates blindness to the lived experience of the fat person.

Use of the couch in Jungian analysis is less common than in traditional psychoanalysis. But I wanted to try it so for some months I lay on the couch during sessions. The couch was old, and creaked, and groaned when I lay down on it. The couch itself seemed to be rebuking me for being too much, seemed to be threatening to break under my weight. I abandoned the couch for many months. When I wanted to return to it, he told me that I couldn't, that it would not hold me. It didn't register with me that he was saying the couch was broken. I heard what he said as meaning I, only I, could not lie on it because I was too heavy. That it had simply broken down did not occur to me. I was humiliated, ashamed, and furious because I thought I was being told that I was too much for it. I felt that he was rejecting me as I am by having a couch that couldn't hold me. I felt as if the space that could hold all of me had shrunk. Yet as we wound our way through the field of land mines surrounding this issue of fat and my body, he was open to hearing my experience, which is a major determinative factor in creating a positive therapeutic environment. In a second analysis with him years later when I was ready to deal with my body, I asked him to read Judith Moore's book, *Fat Girl*, which is a brutally frank memoir of her life as a fat child and woman. He read it. That mattered.

The Jungian approach to therapy employs the belief that both patient and therapist change in the course of the therapy. The patient on an unconscious level functions as therapist to the unconscious patient in the therapist. Jung describes it:

> In any effective psychological treatment the doctor is bound to influence the patient; but this influence can only take place if the patient has a reciprocal influence on the doctor. You can exert no influence if you are not susceptible to influence. (Jung, 1966, p. 71)

In the prevailing mode of therapy used today, cognitive behavioral therapy, the Jungian view most definitely does not apply. But in a model where both patient and therapist are in the soup together, both do change. In the case of dealing with fat, it is the fat patient who confronts the cultural fat complex and in that process dares to confront her therapist's attitudes and beliefs. She can begin to tell her story in her own voice. Jane Burka asks:

> If my body is present and significant for me and for my patients, but remains outside the discourse of the therapy, what kind of taboo have my patients and I created? What deadness is insured and what vitality is precluded? Will the therapy have to take a skewed direction in order to protect my anxieties as the therapist, just as the infant learns to develop a pathological way to cope with a mother's anxieties? (Burka, 2001, p. 274)

A great deal of change is needed for it to become the usual for a fat therapy patient to encounter a therapist free of an agenda about her patient's weight. She should be able to expect to be asked what she wants to work on, what her own goals in therapy are and not to be subject to an agenda that she could/should lose at least a little or a lot of weight. The therapist needs to be willing to hear and accept that her fat patient may not see her weight per se as the problem in her life, even as she experiences the negative effects of stigma and bias, that it may be that the pain of living in a stigmatized body is what she most needs and wants help with. Most importantly that it not be the therapist's agenda that sets the course of the therapy. In a book published in the late 80s, *Fat Oppression and Psychotherapy*, Laura Brown identifies a problem: "… while it was acceptable for clients to be fat women, therapists as so-called models of good functioning, we're required to stay thin" (Brown, 1989, p. 26).

The end to the domination of the cultural fat complex in the field of psychotherapy is nowhere in sight because the field is as much in the grip of that complex as the culture at large is. It falls to fat patients, and fat therapists, to find our voices to protest and begin to force that change. That would bring a Stonewall moment perhaps. Or so I hope.

CHAPTER FOUR

Dancing with Marion Woodman:
searching for meaning

Jung's analytical psychology forms the foundation of my work and my thinking about the psyche, psychic life, dreams, therapy, symptoms. In my Jungian world, I accept that we develop symptoms when we are stuck in old patterns and fail to integrate creative potentials within our personality. Symptoms are not to be avoided or downplayed; their meaning needs to be discovered in order for healing to take place. In that way of understanding life, I accept that my fat is meaningful, but does that also mean that my fat is a symptom of something, that it is not merely one of several basic ways of being, of type of body? Perhaps being fat gives rise to a variety of symptoms? Or maybe it is the experience of being fat, of the daily trauma of membership in a stigmatized group that creates symptoms?

In general the fat acceptance community rejects any of what they see as pathologising psychological bases for being fat, but I believe it is a big mistake to entirely discard the reality that body is influenced by mind. I do agree that being fat is not in itself a mark of psychopathology, that neither physical nor mental health can be determined by a look at body size. So how do we explore and understand the meaning of fat without blaming or pathologising? How do we understand what fat and being fat symbolise without conflating that with cause or symptom?

Before I understood the dimensions of the cultural fat complex, I wanted to find the cause for my fat because if I could find the cause, I could either transform myself into the thin person I was allegedly supposed to be or I could become free of blame if, in fact, the cause were beyond individual control. As I wrote earlier, I read and tried on every theory, biological and psychological, that I could find. But I kept balking at believing deep within myself that my weight was solely and truly my responsibility. Accepting that argument, the emotional theory, meant that I was accepting, as the culture would have me believe, that I have no right to exist as a fat person, that my moral and civic obligation is to do everything in my power to become not-fat so that I could achieve the right to exist in the world without suffering judgment, stigma, and all the indignities to which fat people are subject.

It is a struggle to separate symptom from pathology and allow meaning. Is my fat a symptom and of what? Callan suggests "... what we keep in the shadows, in a place of forgetfulness, turns to symptom" (Callan, 2004, p. 7). So, perhaps it is in the silence about fat experience and the consequent symptoms where we can find meaning.

There is a very thin line in the space between "either" and "or," a razor-thin edge where both/and exists. In this narrow space, which is so very hard to hold on to, causation is not a settled matter and in a basic way not relevant because chasing cause is accepting the underlying assumption that fat people are aberrant and should not exist. It is not a matter of either biology (soma) or emotion (psyche) but the place where biology meets emotion. And where there is no magical solution. In this place, I know I am fat because I came with a body, which among other things, has genetic instructions for being efficient about storing energy. And in this place, fat also has meaning in my life, exists meaningfully—that is the Jungian voice in me that knows there is a meaningful basis alongside the physical.

It is a very difficult space to hold. I find myself falling into very concrete, materialistic and linear thinking resisting looking at meaning because I do not want to accept that my complexes are a causative factor in my fat. The evidence on the side of biology is too strong for me to accept that had I a different, less negative mother, for example, I would have been thin. And yet, I cannot escape either the role fat plays in my life and the meaning it has for me, or how it relates to my mother complex and so much else in my psyche. If I am to hold mind and body together, I cannot privilege body at the expense of mind, I cannot hold to a purely biological cause and reject any emotional one. Surely the shame that is there right under the surface is as much a part of fat as are the genes disposing me to be fat. It is easy to see how a person can get caught in this loop. I can see now that wanting to understand what *causes* me to be fat was in fact symptomatic of being caught in the cultural fat complex, because in wanting to find cause, I was by implication also seeking cure.

Years ago I attended a workshop led by Marion Woodman, a prominent Jungian analyst and author. Woodman came to prominence in the Jungian and New Age worlds in the 80s with her books about women. I had read all of her books and was eager to hear her. We spent the day in a large room in suburban Boston, around 100 of us, all women, come to hear her talk about women, and bodies, and life. I vividly remember the image on the cover of her then new book, *The Ravaged Bridegroom*—that hand reaching up from below caught my breath and made me anxious. I remember feeling disappointed in the workshop, though today I don't remember why.

At the end, Woodman wanted us all to get up and dance. The girl who tried to teach herself ballet, who never learned how to follow in ballroom dance, that girl did not dance, especially in a large group. I stayed seated, hoping to escape notice in the crowd. But she would have none of that and came over and told me to join the dance. I quietly refused. She persisted. I felt badgered and angry. I heard that "No!" from me again, this time with a steel edge. She backed away. That is what I remember from the day I spent with her—that I said No, echoing the very first thing I remember saying to my mother when I stomped my foot and said, "I won't."

Marion Woodman is to date the only Jungian to write about weight and eating in more than a passing way. I read her books *The Owl Was a Baker's Daughter* and *Addiction to Perfection* soon after they were published in the early 1980s. I was searching for answers and hungrily seized on her books hoping to find within them an explanation, a way to understand my body and, of course, to become thin. I so wanted there to be a Jungian answer to my questions about my body. I tried to take in her arguments but they did not resonate with me. I read and re-read what she said but kept feeling she was not talking about me. I said, "No," just as I did when I refused to dance at her workshop.

Woodman says "It takes great courage to break with one's past history and stand alone" (Woodman, 1982, p. 28) And she is right. When I came to her books, I was caught in the Fantasy of Thinness. I thought:

> When I am thin, my husband will love me more.
> When I am thin, I will be happy and confident.
> When I am thin, I will learn to play tennis.
> When I am thin, I will have more friends.
> When I am thin, I will be more successful.

I struggled and managed to give up that fantasy. Because I realized I had a choice—to accept myself as I am or continue to put off living the life I wanted until some mythic time when I became thin. If I hadn't made that choice, I would still be waiting for life to begin for me.

You know the story about the creation of Michelangelo's David? Where he chipped away all of the stone that was not David until he appeared? Well, that is not how it is for me, for those of us who are fat, not really. We wish that it were so but there is no sculptor who will come and somehow magically chip away all the excess flesh and out of the raw material of our bodies will emerge the real us, the thin version, the one who has been inside trying to get out all along. She just isn't there. Despite what Marion Woodman and many others believe, the woman inside is ME, not some thinner other me. To believe in that other thinner me, to believe she is the REAL me is to believe I cannot be me and be fat. It is to believe that this me, this fat me is false, is not really a person.

At the beginning of this project I returned to Woodman's books. I knew I needed to engage her theory, which basically theorizes that fat is symptomatic of several complexes and that working through those complexes in analysis would by implication lead to cessation of disordered eating and weight reduction. In Woodman's theory, there is inside the fat woman, the proverbial thin woman who can be let out. In essence then, fat is a marker for pathology. I knew I had to engage her theory despite my resistance to it in order to credibly put forth my own ideas. I told myself that perhaps there is so little else written by Jungians on the subject of fatness because she said all that needed to be said. I started arguing with her, trying both to find in me the truth of what she says and resisting it. I would read what she wrote and then mentally argue with her. I argued in part to escape the weight of what she is saying; if I can reject part of it, I can reject all of it. I picked and chose passages that I could find reason to reject. I was certain she was wrong. I tried, I really tried to win this intellectual argument. I found others who were critical of her and used them to bolster my resistance.

Still I wanted to explore the meaning of my fat and I knew that meant returning first to Woodman. Had she in fact with her theory said all that needed to be said about fat, at least from the Jungian perspective? Or was she, like most of us, in the grip of the cultural fat complex and unable to see fat as anything other than problematic? I started again, this time making myself more open, working to still the arguments and try to take in what she said. In the end, I do reject an essential element of what she proposes, but I also find myself accepting far more than I ever thought I would, though not in the way she intends. I found my both/and position.

When I read Woodman, I get lost in her clouds of metaphors and my copies of both *The Owl Was a Baker's Daughter* and *Addiction to Perfection* are filled with "what does this mean?" written in the margins as I try to find the nuggets of what she says. Working my way through her books meant I had to work to find those nuggets and engage with her through them.

The Owl was a Baker's Daughter is based on Woodman's thesis presented to the Jung Institute in Zurich. She uses Jung's Word Association Test to try to tease out complexes held in common by her obese subjects. The common word association game that many of us have played where one person says a noun, like "dog," and the next says what comes to mind in association to the word, like "bark" or "cat" is similar to this test. Jung drew on his observation that people connect ideas, feelings, experiences, and information by way of associations and that these associations are linked or grouped and indicate the presence of complexes.

Despite my annoyance that Woodman ties obesity to compulsive eating, she does at least give a nod to other bases for becoming fat—"Endogenous or primary obesity develops from within; exogenous or secondary obesity requires overeating" (Woodman, 1980, p. 7). She does not provide any further thoughts on these differences or how they come to be. Throughout the book, she seems to forget the distinction she draws between endogenous and exogenous obesity and writes as if it all stems from compulsive eating.

Of the complexes Woodman sees as implicated in obesity, the following show the strongest connection, at least judging from the way she reports her data: Mother, Father, Anger/Aggression, Food. Of Mother, Father and Anger/Aggression. Mother is actually the one with the strongest connection. In fact she all but says that the Mother Complex is at the heart of it all.

Looking at her work with a psychologist's eye, I see a study with many methodological flaws, among them a very small sample and no criteria given for how these women were selected or what definition of obesity she employed. Though certainly some fat people are compulsive eaters, there is no real support for the way she ties them together as a given. Nor is her assumption that anorexia and obesity are closely related supportable. Anorexia is an eating disorder; in fact one can be both fat and anorexic. As Saguy points out

> ... overweight and obesity have been defined broadly to include anyone with a BMI over 25 or 30, respectively, regardless of body composition or health status, while anorexia has been defined quite narrowly. Specifically, the APA defines anorexia as the refusal to maintain body weight at or above a minimally "normal weight" for age and height (85 percent of "expected" weight), fear of gaining weight or becoming "fat," denial of the gravity of one's low body weight, and, in post-menarchal females, amenorrhea. (Saguy, 2012, p. 96)

Many, perhaps even Woodman, assume obesity is also an eating disorder, or at least the result of one. It is sometimes presented as Eating Disorder, Not Otherwise Specified (EDNOS) though at best that is arguable. Weight is a physical characteristic. Obesity has a rather loose definition but is not a psychiatric disorder. As a piece of psychological research, her study is of questionable value, but she does at least attempt to explore the issues in a Jungian framework, something no one else has done. She acknowledges that what she identifies as true of obese women can easily be seen as true for most women, that much of what her obese subjects said could easily have been made by any woman. But then she asserts that "Obesity is one of the chief symptoms of neurosis in the Western world" (Woodman, 1980, p. 89). Woodman falls prey to confirmation bias in seeing in her very limited sample evidence of what she already believes.

Given these flaws, which are serious, still I want to explore the applicability and utility of her theory, if only because her assumption that obesity is symptomatic of neurosis is deeply ingrained in analytical psychology and psychoanalysis. Were I to sidestep engaging her theory it too easily could be construed as prime evidence that I am doing so defensively and thus enable any other thoughts I have to be dismissed. Using the method of autoethnography, "an approach to research and writing that seeks to describe and systematically analyze personal experience in order to understand cultural experience"(Ellis, Adams, & Bochner, 2010), I will explore the first complex she cites, Mother, in light of her work and my own history and make of myself a kind of single case study. I will use passages from her book which illustrate her theory and then explore what she says in light of my own history, in some ways as if we were in analysis together and I were associating to what she says. Of course, actual analytic sessions would not flow this way. The italicized quotes which follow are from *The Owl Was A Baker's Daughter* unless otherwise noted.

CHAPTER FIVE

Woodman, my mother, and me

In what follows, imagine if you will that you are reading notes from an analysis, with Marion Woodman, voiced via italicized quotes from her writing about obesity, as the analyst and I, the analysand. She makes an observation or interpretation and I respond, defending, resisting, and sometimes accepting what she says.

> **Woodman:** *I think eating disorders are related to a problem with the mother. Mother is related to nourishment, cherishing, sweetness—food is a metaphor for mother* (Peay, 1992, p. 10).

Am I fat because of my mother? If my mother had loved and wanted me, had held me and let me know she wanted me, would I be thin? This is where I usually balk and become very literal. Something in me wants to shout "NO!" when I come to this point.

A photo of me with my daughter, taken when she was about three months old, shows us delighting in each other. It is so different from any of me with my mother. I am laughing and she is laughing and we are saying I love you with our eyes—that isn't there for me with my mother. She was stiff, and sad, and far away. In a picture of my mother and me, taken in 1946 when I was around a month old, she seems almost to be trying to hold her body away from me. There are no photos of us in which we make eye contact and rarely are we ever even looking in the same direction. In contrast to the pictures of me with my children where our shared joy is evident, there is a sense of sadness and distance in those of me with my mother.

My mother was never fat. At five foot, seven, she ranged from average weight to quite thin. She was pretty though she rarely looked happy. Even when she was smiling, she carried a sense of sadness and seemed far away.

From the beginning, my mother and I had struggles about eating and not eating. I learned that I could make her furious by refusing to eat—I may have learned it as a baby. As a young child of three or four, I sat at the table after everyone had left, singing to myself and refusing to eat all or some of what she had served. My chair faced the windows. In summer I liked trying to stay up until the sun went down. She would start by telling me I had to stay at the table until I ate everything on my plate. But when she saw I was perfectly content to sit there and amuse myself, she would begin to scold and yell at me until finally she would take me off to bed. I remember feeling I had won. Not doing what she wanted me to do made me powerful. I didn't eat the food I didn't like and I got to stay up later. She couldn't make me eat. I had control.

In the baby book she kept about me, she notes very little other than her struggles to get me to eat. Again and again she noted taking me to the doctor, determined that there was something wrong with me. Though she saw me as not thriving, the measurements she recorded in that book show I was developing normally. What I was not getting was her, was her body, being held and nuzzled and loved by a mother who wanted me. I imagine myself sad and furious with her. I could get even with her by not eating. By not eating I could make her feel as frustrated and inadequate as I felt. By not eating I could keep her from mothering me in this way as she kept me from being mothered in other ways.

In the years before I was five, my mother was ill much of the time. It was my father or my brothers who cooked—Franco-American canned spaghetti or shredded wheat or cream chipped beef and I hated it all. To this day I shudder inwardly at the very thought of those foods. Or sometimes it was my grandmother or my aunt or my godmother. I was picky. They all spent time trying to persuade me to eat what they offered. It seems a great deal of time was spent on what I ate and getting me to eat.

She was often sick. Other people came to take care of her and of me. Sometimes she was away in the hospital. Sometimes at home in her room. Or they would take me away to my grandmother's house and I wouldn't see her for a long time. Or to my godparents' house. Where was home anyway? When I think of the home of my childhood, no one place comes to mind, though my grandmother's house comes closest. I had no control over any of that, of where I stayed or who took care of me but I could refuse to eat. Eating or not eating was the way I could protest and make them worry about me and fuss over me and see me. I could have some power and control by not eating.

Am I fat because of my mother? Is there any way to separate my fat from her? My earliest memory of her is from when I was about two. I remember stomping my foot and saying loudly, "I WON'T!"—the very thing I did again years later with Marion Woodman. She didn't like that at all. But it is emblematic of how we were with each other, so often in opposition to each other, resisting each other. I learned this nonsense poem from her—

> One bright day in the middle of the night,
> Two dead boys got up to fight.
> Back-to-back they faced one another,
> Drew their swords and shot each other.

Somehow that describes us. The mother who was so unhappy, who had wanted to leave her husband and then got pregnant again, right after the War ended. I can imagine that she must have felt trapped, a baby again after so long—twelve years separate me from my next older brother—a baby just when she was hoping to leave and have a new life, a life with a man who would love and want her. And then that baby turned out to be a girl. Adored by grandparents, named by my father who said he always wanted a little girl, cute, precocious, while she, my mother, was ill. I was the one thing in her life that could steal attention away from her at the same time that I demanded from her and defied her. So we fought and struggled always for power and control.

> She told me I was a mistake.
> She told me everything was fine until I came along.
> She told me that I could fool everyone else, but I couldn't fool her; she knew what I was really like.

She told me I thought too much of myself.

She told me no one would want me because of the way I treated her.

She told me no man would ever want to marry me.

She told me I would never amount to anything.

She told me I was nothing but trouble from the day I was born.

She told me she was happy, that everything was fine until I was born.

Though I argued with her and defied her, the steady drumbeat of those messages from her found its way deep inside.

I would sneak into her room when she was sick and sleeping and climb on the bed next to her and with my fingers try to open her eyes. Because I wanted her to wake up, see me, be with me, play with me. Because I needed her. But when she did wake up, she was not the mother I wanted, the mother I needed. She didn't hold me. She didn't play with me. I remember her telling my teenaged brother to read to me or draw for me. "Amuse her," she would tell him and he would, grudgingly, muttering angry things under his breath. He would draw for a little while and then tell me I'd better not complain. But I didn't want him anyway. I wanted her and she wouldn't do those things with me. The mother I wanted and needed remained asleep and oblivious to me and my desire.

I hid from her, watched her from under the table. I wanted to be close but not too close. I wanted to be able to see her. I needed to keep her in sight. I had my dolls and stuffed animals with me under the drop-leaf dining room table. I could see her in the kitchen, watch her, and keep an eye on her. I don't remember doing it, but I blinded several of those toys—my panda, a stuffed Pluto dog, and a lamb—I twisted off their button eyes, peeled off Pluto's eyes, ears, and tail. My mother would replace them and I would do it again. Taking their eyes off was one of the stories I have told about myself but I never thought about why I did it. What was it that I didn't want them to see? I remember the sensation of twisting the button eyes off my panda but not what was going on or what I felt when I did it. The memory is just not there. What I remember is being both afraid of her and wanting her. I think about my own daughter when she was a little girl and then I can imagine that I was furious with my mother. In the little that I do remember, I see the traces of that fury. I imagine that I took out that anger on my animals because

I couldn't show her what I felt. I hurt them as she hurt me. Sixty-five years later and I see that stuffed Pluto on a shelf across the room. His ears and tail are gone, twisted off by an angry child who could not take out her anger any place else, his eyes made of felt with black pupils painted on, replacing the eyes I had peeled off so many times before. He carries my scars.

I remember being in the bathroom after she got out of the tub. I would sit on the toilet seat and watch her get dressed. If I stayed quiet, she would let me stay and watch her. I can still smell the April Violets powder she would sprinkle on her body. She didn't seem at all self-conscious about letting me see her naked. I noticed her thick brown pubic hair and that her breasts sagged. When I remember now, knowing she was in her mid-thirties then, I am surprised by how old her body looked, sagging in her belly and hips. I can remember the scars on her flank from when she had surgery of some kind. I wanted to reach over and touch those scars, red lines on her flank. But I didn't. I knew she would get angry if I did. If I stayed quiet, I could stay.

One night, when I was no more than four, I remember coming out of my room. I have no idea why I was up. The house was quiet. The lights were on in the living room. I saw my mother. I don't think she saw me. She was sitting in a chair in the living room, smoking and looking off into space. I watched her for a long time. She was lost in her thoughts. Perhaps she was angry with my father for not being home—was he away then or just late? I never considered saying anything, interrupting her, because she would have gotten angry with me, spanked me perhaps for being up. She seemed tired and sad and far away.

These memories are like snapshots, without words. Vivid images that flash on the screen of my mind. What was I feeling those times under the table or in the bathroom or that night as I watched her? Though I have no memory for what I felt as I watched my mother, I can imagine that I was feasting on her with my eyes, able to be visually close to her as I was not able to be otherwise. I could keep track of her, alert to changes in her mood, and at the same time take her in. Perhaps taking the eyes off my animals was an expression of my rage that I could only have her by watching. I hit a strong resistance in myself when I try to understand that act more deeply, to see the sadism that it was.

She often said she thought I had been "vaccinated with a phonograph needle." When she and I were alone, I talked to myself because she didn't talk to me much at all. My talking must have felt like an assault on her. I understand because that's how my son's talking felt to me when he was very small. He talked and talked and talked and demanded that I pay attention to him. He wanted my attention. He would put his hands on either side of my face and make me look into his eyes and talk to me. I was depressed, hardly able to be present. And he talked and talked to me. I must have been like that with her. Open your eyes. See me. Play with me. Want me. Love me. Make me real. Give me your approval. Make me special. Tell me I exist, that I am here. I talked to hear myself and know I was there, as if otherwise I was substanceless, fleeting, evanescent.

I don't remember her saying much to me about my weight before I was a teenager, at least not directly. But there was something in her tone that told me she did not like how I looked. She took me to the doctor for a diet when I was nine. I felt ashamed, too big. I had to write down everything I ate—I can see the notebook I had, a long narrow spiral notebook, I wrote in pencil. The doctor was a woman. I did as I was supposed to. My body didn't. I remained chubby.

Then she didn't want me to wear my glasses—I think she connected it to being less desirable because she told me, "Men don't make passes at girls who wear glasses." I was nine and had no idea what she meant but I knew it wasn't good. I was quite nearsighted but she would say, "Oh you don't really need those glasses" as if somehow they were a blight on her image because they marked me as defective. I can't remember her saying, in words, much else to me about how I looked. But I could feel in other ways that she disapproved of my appearance. My weight. My hair. My glasses. The way my blouse would come untucked. In short, she disapproved of everything about me.

When I was little, not eating made me powerful with her. Made me stronger than she was. So why didn't I become anorexic? I could have made her afraid, afraid I would die, like I wanted to when I stood under the icy water in the rain when I was five and thought she'd be sorry when I got sick and died. But she told me so many times I was a mistake, I already thought she wanted me gone. That five year old who got so angry with her, who stood under the downspout on an icy rainy day wanted to punish her, to hurt her. There is cold anger in becoming too big to erase, too big a mistake to ignore.

When I was four, I had my tonsils out. She fretted that I was a picky eater and still worried about what and how I ate. The doctor told my mother to watch, soon I would eat her out of house and home. I remember those words and how strange that idea seemed. Is that what

I wanted to do? I don't remember eating more. I was a picky eater before my tonsils were removed; I was a picky eater afterwards. But I did begin to become fat, become too much to erase like other mistakes.

Something else was happening at the same time. My father was in the Army National Guard. That same summer that I had my tonsils taken out, my father's unit was activated at the outbreak of the Korean War and he began to be away for longer and longer periods of time. I began to grow fat then, when he was gone, leaving me with her, alone with her and one of my brothers for months at a time. He was gone when I had my tonsils out.

The power in fat is to be other than what she wanted me to be. She wanted me to be thin, pretty, charming, and smart. She wanted me to be popular and to have lots of friends. To be all the things she wasn't able to be. She wanted me to have lots of boyfriends. She wanted me to become a doctor and for quite a while I thought I wanted that too, but along the way I was drawn instead to psychology. She never spoke to me about my choice after I told her I was changing my major other than to tell me that I was disappointing a lot of people in choosing not to be a doctor. In fact no one in my family has ever spoken of the fact that I became a psychotherapist, as if to do so would open up a family wound otherwise held in secret.

Maybe by being fat, I could show everyone how hungry I was, how huge was my need, and somehow show it to be her failing. I wanted to hurt her. I wanted to destroy her. In my fury at her for not wanting me, for not loving me, instead of dying, I became fat, too much to not see. I rubbed her face in my presence. My very presence was an expression of my hostility and defiance and hate for her. A Pyrrhic victory. It sounds willful but it wasn't really a decision, wasn't a conscious goal. It was a way to survive, to protect myself from the corrosive relationship I had with her. Even as I can see the link between being fat and my fury at her, can see meaning it seems to have had, the mechanism for it puzzles me. The fury, fear, yearning, and hostility of a little girl turns into fat? My mind boggles at this. The scientist in me wants to know how this happens. It is easier to wonder about that than to take in and feel its truth. At the same time I can just glimpse the wonder of it, that I found perhaps the best way possible to resist her, by becoming too much for her to not see.

Woodman: *I think eating disorders are related to a problem with the mother. Mother is related to nourishment, cherishing, sweetness—food is* *a metaphor for mother … It's a longing for the archetypal mother. The sweetness, the cherishing, the acceptance, the mirroring by the missing mother-I mean mother with a big "M". Because this is not just a longing for the personal mother, but a longing for the Mother Goddess, a being in whom you can have total trust.* (Peay, 1992, p. 11)

I yearned for my mother, that mother who would talk with me and do things with me and love me. It isn't that everything between us was negative. I have a sprinkling of positive memories too—making May baskets with her, birthday parties when I was seven and when I was ten. Clothes of hers she gave me for playing dress-up. Going over lists of words as I prepared for spelling bees. These memories are like sprinkles on top of bitter ice cream, nice to look at but unable to cover the taste of the actual dish. The dominant tone between us was one of strain, of a mixture of yearning, hostility, and unpredictability because I never knew what would make her turn, make her angry and that eclipsed for the most part what positive times we had. Once when I was especially miserable when I was a teenager, I confided in her about my loneliness and my feelings of not belonging. And she listened. Then in a matter of hours she turned everything I had confided back on me as proof that everything she said about me—that no one would like me—was true. After that I knew better than to be drawn in by her.

Not only was my mother negative, she was also disturbed. She was paranoid. She was hypochondriacal. My first husband once character-ized her as speaking in concept salad, with jumbled references that made no sense to others, but which, because I was with her more than anyone else, I understood. Her irrationality and paranoid thinking frustrated me, even enraged me. That I could understand her terrified me because deep inside I feared what it meant about me, that because I understood her I too was mad though I kept it at bay with logic and rationality. Being alone with her felt like being in Alice in Wonderland, a story I always hated. It was never knowing which way was up or what she would do. Feeling this, remembering makes my stomach churn and I feel dizzy. The feeling is of being disoriented all the time, things mov-ing in unpredictable directions so I have to grab hold of something and hang on in order not to be sucked into it. It is like trying to walk on a floor that is undulating in all directions in a room with fun house mirrors for walls. All I wanted was for her to be normal, to be rational.

I always wanted to scream at her to please make sense, please stop the craziness because it was so disturbing and frightening. I became cold in order not to let her touch me. I had to keep her out somehow.

I couldn't let go of wanting her, yet I was eager to get away from her, so eager that when I was choosing a college, the first criterion was that it be at least 400 miles away from her, too far away for her and my father to drop in without warning. Though I was eager to leave, I kept the hope that someday somehow it would all change. Every time I anticipated seeing her, I imagined we would go out to lunch together or go shopping or do something together like other mothers and daughters did, like I do with my now adult daughter. We would talk, talk about ourselves, about life. We would be interested in each other. And every time within a few minutes of being with her, I was angry and had that crazy feeling that I was fighting for reality against her madness and irrationality. Within minutes of being with her, I wanted her gone again. And when she left, the yearning would return.

We danced a tarantella, possessed by the spider of poisonous love and hate and rage and yearning. I was confused about her—I asked her so many times or maybe I only asked once and it just seems like I did it many times, but I asked her if she loved me because I really did not know and needed to hear her say she did. She wouldn't say the words. She would look at me scornfully and flick her hand at me as if to wave me away, and say "Don't be foolish." What did that mean—it was foolish to ask? I was foolish to think she did? Or did not? I still don't know. I don't remember telling her I loved her either. The dance continued until she died.

She sent me a letter many years later, when I was forty. She wrote it on my birthday. In the letter she told me that I had kept her waiting in the hottest summer on record—I was twenty-four days late, something she never tired of telling me—and then she wrote that I must have wanted to stay inside her where I was nice and cozy, next to her heart. I forgot about that letter until I was writing this. There was a kind of wistful tone to the letter, though as with most of the long long letters she wrote me, it was mostly filled with complaints about my father, her doctors, neighbors, and paranoid rants. But I remember that one little bit, feeling touched for a moment because it was the first time she talked about my being late as something other than an inconvenience for her. That she saw me as having been warm and cozy and wanting to stay inside her was something I had never heard from her before. Maybe that was the only time the two of us were happy with each other, in the months before I was born.

> **Woodman:** ... *where the primal relationship is disturbed, the child blames itself, and being unloved becomes synonymous with being abnormal, guilty, alone.* (Woodman, 1980, p. 95)

I understand this, about the effects of a disturbed relationship with the mother, but is it not the case regardless of weight and size? My relationship with my mother was disturbed and negative from the beginning. I believe this to be an instance of correlation not causation. The relationship was negative from the beginning, long before I became fat, long before I was born even. And I must also admit that becoming fat also insulated me, expressed defiance and perhaps signaled that something was awry.

My mother sought to control my body, just as she tried to control everything else about me. When I was a baby and rather thin, or so my mother said, I was given a diphtheria, pertussis, and tetanus (DPT) shot in my thigh. I don't know if this was the usual practice but she attributed it to my small size. For some reason an abscess formed at the injection site. It persisted over a period of months and the treatment of it left a deep scar on my leg.

I started kindergarten at my grandmother's where my mother, my brother, and I were to live until we could join my father in Japan where he and my other brother were on active duty with the Army. My brother and my grandfather did not get along so after Christmas we moved back to Connecticut so he could finish his junior year at the high school there and be with his friends. But this move took me away from my grandparents and the school that I loved so I was not happy. We lived in a small apartment where I shared a bedroom with my mother. I hated it.

I walked to my new school, walked up a steep hill. My dog would walk with me and then be there when I was ready to walk home again. I did not like the new school. I didn't like my new teacher. I complained to my mother that walking up the hill made my leg hurt, hoping maybe I could go back to my other school, to my grandmother's.

My mother seized on this complaint and took me to the doctor and demanded a referral to a surgeon. I felt trapped and scared. I didn't know how to tell them that my leg was okay. The surgeon agreed with her that the scar tissue in my leg should be removed and the muscle repaired and the procedure was scheduled.

Two days before I was to be operated on, we visited friends who were in the process of replacing the hearth in their living room. A rug covered the opening where the hearth had been. My mother warned me not to step back but as I turned to look at her I accidentally stepped on the rug and fell though the floor, landing in a barrel in the cellar. I was terrified. I just missed landing on a table saw. The entire left side of my body was scraped and bleeding. Our friend carried me upstairs and started to wash the scrapes. My mother's face was red. She was angry and grabbed my arm and started scolding me for being careless. She was furious that this meant the surgery would have to be rescheduled as I had scraped the same side that was to be operated on. Our friends made her back off and admonished her for being too hard on me and for not recognizing that I was scared. I was held and comforted by them. My father was in Japan. Surgery was delayed for two weeks.

When I was a little girl, I was often sick with ear and throat infections. When I got sick, she became attentive in a way that she was not ordinarily. That attention came close enough to what I yearned for that I reveled in it. Until I was in seventh grade, I used to miss twenty or more days of school a year, at home with illnesses of one kind or another, some real, some manufactured. I stayed at home with books and magazines and she would fix foods to tempt me and generally act solicitously toward me.

There was a danger to her care though. Perhaps she verged on Munchausen by proxy because when I was sick, it was not enough for it to be some simple illness. When I had a string of gastrointestinal illnesses when I was ten, she insisted to the doctor that I had appendicitis, and she demanded that my appendix be removed. Each time I developed one of those illnesses, and I recall at least three or four instances that year, she would take me to the doctor and make her demand. But because the symptoms were neither conclusive nor sufficiently serious, there was no surgery. She seemed disappointed. I overheard a close friend, who was a doctor, tell my father that he should get my mother some help because she was pushing so hard to convince someone I needed to have my appendix removed.

When I developed cramps with my period when I was around twelve, she was certain they indicated some serious problem and took me to a gynecologist and insisted he do a pelvic exam to find out what was wrong; when he said I was fine, she was angry and said she thought he was not a very good doctor.

Soon thereafter any cold became mononucleosis to her and she would demand that blood work be done, certain I had some illness if not mono. Something in her growing attachment to my health or rather illness began to feel uncomfortable to me. I no longer wanted to stay home even when I was really sick. From the middle of seventh grade on, I never voluntarily stayed home from school due to illness. I would hide any symptoms and act as if all were well and go to school. I missed a week in eighth grade when I was sent home because I had a high fever and the flu. In all of high school, I missed no school. In no longer staying home with her, I was giving up the care she would show me then, but more importantly it helped me move away from her.

My analyst once suggested that my mother saw me as a kind of narcissistic extension of herself, that she merged with and identified with my body as something negative, something sick. My body, in its very shape and size bespeaks my need to protect my core from her. As Anita Greene writes of her mother,

> For the first time I grasped the connection between my negative mother complex and how the body had accommodated and responded to its intrusive and controlling energy. I had moved back, dug in my heels, tightened up the spine in a kind of passive but stubborn resistance to anything mother might do. The most disquieting aspect of this instinctual portrait of myself was how it reflected the stubborn and defensive way I approached many present life situations ... The way we carry ourselves is who we are. (Greene, 2001, p. 567)

My mother's preoccupation with her own health was even greater than with mine. For my first four years she was ill most of the time but then she recovered or seemed to and for a number of years she was as normal as she ever was in my life. In those years she played bridge, she participated in the Officer's Wives Club and PTA. She was a room mother and a Brownie Scout leader. She read books and had friends. She and my father went out together and did things together. But just as her preoccupation with my health became dark as I approached my teens, her own psychosomatic concerns also intensified. I experienced her obsession with her medications and her illnesses, real and imagined, and her constant talk about doctors as indications of her madness and as I did with other aspects of her irrational or illogical behavior, I argued with her about it and was scornful toward her desire to get us to pay attention. When her own mother died, when I was not quite fourteen and we lived in Germany, she left all of that normal way of being behind her. She withdrew from social activities. She stopped reading or playing bridge. She and my father stopped having a social life. She retreated entirely into herself and her preoccupation with her health became intense to the exclusion of nearly everything else. Her preoccupation with her health and her body made me less attentive to my own. And her identification with my body as something negative, as sick surely fed my own rejecting feelings about my body. I became less connected to my own body and more to my mind. My body seemed most important to me because it carried my head.

When I was in high school, we lived in a small town in Pennsylvania where my father was one of only fifty Army personnel and there was none of the support structures that had been so helpful to me earlier. We lived in a small house outside of town. There was no public transportation and my mother did not drive. Just as she retreated into her inner world, my world narrowed. All I had outside of home was school. My social life and activities narrowed along with the shrinking she did of her own life.

Body

Woodman: … *body image in some way precedes and determines the body structure. How the psychic sphere is reflected in her body is a question which the obese woman must face. The child absorbs the attitudes of others toward her body.* (Woodman, 1980, p. 96)

When I was nine, I wanted to learn ballet. I begged my mother to let me take a class. She told me no, that I was too fat for ballet. So I got a book from the library, a book that showed the five basic positions for feet and hands. When my mother wasn't home, I would stand in front of the mirror and try to teach myself ballet. I wanted so much to be a graceful and beautiful dancer. But of course, there were limits to what I could teach myself. I practiced those five foot positions and hand positions again and again, trying to imagine myself a ballerina. What I saw in that mirror was my chubby body and lack of grace, just like she said. Whenever I remember that—standing in front of the mirror in the hall and trying so hard to teach myself ballet, I feel a deep sadness. That I was trying so hard to give myself something I wanted and needed from her—support and encouragement to develop a stronger better sense of myself—something she just would not, could not give me.

Then, at my mother's insistence, I took a course in ballroom dancing and etiquette. She was certain this was how I would become graceful and ladylike. I was terrible at dancing; I just couldn't get the hang of following. I didn't know how to let the boy lead, to feel the music, to let go, give up control and allow him to take charge of the dance. It is something I have yet to learn, though in my dreams I am able do it—to let go, feel the music, and dance, my partner leading. And if I can do that in my dreams, perhaps I can do it in waking life.

Woodman sees fat as armor against sexuality. For me the problem and the armor, came before fat. My body, fat or not, became the armor against being hurt deep inside where my most vulnerable self lived. My body became the shell around this vulnerable, needy me. I have never been very comfortable being touched. I don't remember my mother touching me with affection. All I remember is touch from disapproval or punishment or intrusion. When she would comb my hair, she would yank at snarls. When I would cry and tell her that she was hurting me, she would tell me to be quiet or she would give me something to cry about. Or she would slap me because she didn't like something I said or did. Or spank me because she was angry. Or grab my arms and squeeze them in her fury, while telling me "I'm going to shake you until your teeth rattle." Touch from her was too often accompanied by pain.

At least since I was a teenager, when touched, I imagine the other person experiences my body with distaste or disgust and so I brace myself against that. I pull myself way inside myself, as if I could pull myself away from my skin, from my own surface and retreat to some deep inner place too far inside to be touched or hurt as I couldn't pull away from my mother. Life in my mind is much kinder. I am confident about being smart and able to think. I could shine in school. I could lose myself in books. But in my body, I never felt secure. I do not enjoy massage. A few years ago, I decided to try massage because so many people

I knew really loved it. I found a massage therapist that I knew and felt comfortable with and I went to her every two weeks for a year. It wasn't bad but neither did it ever come to feel good.

Sexuality

Woodman: *The woman who has not found herself in her own body is dependent on a man to help her to be born on this earth, and is therefore inclined to project her Self onto the man she loves.* (Woodman, 1980, p. 25)

Sex has always been a mystery to me. My mother never said anything to me about it. I never saw my parents be physically affectionate with each other. They didn't kiss or touch each other. They slept in twin beds. They did not express affection verbally either. As my friends began to be interested in boys and talk about kissing and touching, I didn't really understand. I was interested in boys, but what I was wanting was to be like the other girls, to be desired like they were and I always felt I was not. My friends had crushes on movie stars and rock stars and I didn't get it. It was a whole part of being a teenage girl that I was outside of. I read *Seventeen*, which was *the* magazine for teenage girls, but I didn't really relate to the things others seemed preoccupied with. I remember when I was in high school, thinking that this "French kissing" I heard about was like in the movies when Charles Boyer would start with a kiss to the woman's hand and then move up her arm. I had no idea what petting was or necking or any of the other things friends talked about meant. But I could never let on that I didn't know because I knew that to do so would expose something shameful about me. I have never felt what others describe as being "horny," of wanting sex. What I have felt is wanting to feel wanted. But sex never gave that to me. I imagined, I hoped, I dreamed of finding a man who would teach me, who would awaken desire in me. But it never happened.

I was a wallflower at the dances in junior high. I listened to my friends talk about games of spin the bottle but I was not part of them. I stopped going to the dances. I did not date in high school. In my first year of college I had one date, a blind date. I overheard him tell his friend that he wouldn't have come if he'd known he would be with a dog. I didn't go out again for a year. I was nineteen before I had my first kiss.

In college, I dated Hartmut for several months. I thought he was beautiful and smart and I loved being with him. But I was so terribly inexperienced that I didn't know how to respond to him and he didn't tell me what he wanted. I felt defective because I didn't know what to do. We drifted apart in my junior year.

> **Woodman:** *The obese woman is living out a double bind. Her obses-sion with weight protects her from the conscious confrontation with the opposites—a confrontation which is the only way to the wholeness for which she longs. As a woman, her feminine instinct tells her she must yield, but she is terrified of losing the control which in fact she does not have. At the same time she knows she dare not yield, for fear her worst terrors will be realized: the arms of love are not there. Nor can a loving man be both lover and surrogate mother. Her healing must come through the abyss of the absent feminine.* (Woodman, 1980, p. 100)

There is something, some way I held onto a deep connection to my feminine self, to my femaleness for all of my life. I was always a "girly" girl. My mother used to complain about me that I always insisted on wearing dresses rather than the overalls she wanted me to wear when I played. I loved dresses, especially dresses with pockets and that used to annoy her also because she hated that I would always put my hands in my pockets. She would sew the pockets shut and I would pick the stitches out again to open them. To this day, I love skirts and dresses with pockets and would rather wear a skirt than pants.

My breasts began to develop when I was around nine and I was delighted. I wanted to be a woman. I had baby doll pajamas with a loose ruffled top when I was that age. I used to sometimes pretend I was pregnant or that I had a baby because that was what being, becoming a woman meant to me. From the time I was a very little girl, I loved playing with my dolls and I always knew I wanted to grow up and have children. I never really dreamed of the kind of husband I wanted; it was children I looked forward to.

My mother had hemorrhaged after I was born and had to have a hysterectomy. She left it to school to tell me about menstruation and when in fifth grade they showed a film for mothers to see with their daughters, she stayed home. I had my first period when I was eleven. I was delighted. To me it meant something deep and important. My peri-ods were regular from the start and I marveled at the inner timekeeper they were part of and the connection to the moon. I loved the full moon and the new moon. Even now I track the phases of the moon and try to photograph the full moon if I can. Somewhere when I was young I read that menstrual blood was the weeping of a disappointed womb and that notion fit into my very romantic feelings about what it was to be a woman. I never talked with anyone about those feelings. For me they were secret, sacred, and I knew if I said anything about them to my mother, she would ridicule me for them. Suffering her own wounded feminine, she was unable to celebrate or be open to me and my emerging womanhood. Those feelings became my secret delight in being female and they set me apart somehow from her.

For me, getting married was all about being able to have the children I had so long desired. Left to my own devices, I would have gotten pregnant in that first year, but it was six years later that my first child, my daughter was born. I first had to persuade my husband that the time was right and then when he finally agreed, we had difficulty conceiving. My heart sank as month after month went by with no pregnancy. I feared that some terrible trick had been played on me, that I had faithfully taken my birth control pill every day for all those years for nothing. I became very depressed. We went to a fertility specialist to see what the problem was. We were in the middle of the work-up, just days before I was to have surgery to look at my ovaries, when I missed my period, the first time ever for me. And then a positive pregnancy test. I was elated. I wanted to tell everyone. It was proof that I was a real woman. I called my mother. I wanted her to be excited with me. She coldly told me not to count my chickens before they hatched, which felt to me like a wish that this baby would not survive and be born.

I had problems in that pregnancy. My blood pressure became elevated. I was on partial bed rest. I entered labor two weeks early. At the end of that long labor, when I was more tired than I had ever been, I felt like my whole being narrowed down to some essential core, and all that existed was the effort of trying to push her out. I can remember feeling near the end that I was in a place where even as she was about to be born, death was very close. I hemorrhaged within an hour of her birth, my blood pressure dropped suddenly and very low. I could feel myself fading out. I rang for the nurse. I knew I could die, that something was very wrong. I kept thinking that this was so unfair, that I couldn't die now when I had just had my baby. That was just not right. It took a while but the bleeding was stopped. The birth was very difficult and I hemorrhaged. But I had my baby girl and I was ecstatic. I saw her connected through me to my mother and her mother and all the mothers going back to the beginning and somehow that made being my mother's daughter almost all right. My baby was a wonder.

Two years later I became pregnant again. Again my husband was reluctant. Again I had difficulties with hypertension during the pregnancy. I was placed on strict bed rest for fourteen weeks and there were real questions about whether the baby or I would survive. I was advised that I would not likely survive a subsequent pregnancy and that I should terminate my fertility. My son was born via cesarean section. I had a tubal ligation at that time. I became very depressed afterwards, in no small measure because losing my fertility felt like a terrible blow to myself as a woman. I didn't want more children but I did not want to have that possibility taken from me either. Since I was eleven and had my first period, it was that potential, that possibility of pregnancy that was central to being a woman for me. Losing that, having it taken from me, meant losing something of my deepest self and I mourned the loss. My mother had a hysterectomy soon after my birth. Did she mourn that loss too?

I loved being pregnant, in spite of the fact that both of my pregnancies were complicated and the births difficult. I loved my pregnant body. I felt lush, ripe, and fertile. I was free of feeling shame about being fat when I was pregnant. When I was pregnant I felt connected to the earth and all women. I loved feeling my hard belly; in fact I marveled that my pregnant belly was hard as I had never experienced that before. Inside my body bread and wine were turning into the flesh and blood of another being; transubstantiation was a reality in me. And when I was nursing my babies, I felt kinship with a goddess, a goddess like those painted by Meinrad Craighead in her book *Mother's Songs: Images of God The Mother* (Craighead, 1986)—fecund, lush, amazed at the miracle that I could feed my babies that way and they would grow and thrive. That was my connection to the Great Mother.

I feel and have always felt deeply connected to the wonder of being a woman, of what my woman's body can do, but it has not brought with it that something deeper that Woodman refers to. But just what does that mean, "the feminine principle"? As I sit with it, I feel confused. What is it beyond being connected in this deep way to my body, to my femaleness?

Woodman: *The soul went underground at about the age of one, and the little girl started to perform and be what people wanted her to be about the age of one ... So you've got to allow that one-year-old to catch up, in a spiritual sense, to what she is in her physical body. Then she will be able to relate to men.* (Woodman, 1980, p. 96)

For most of my life I have not been really interested in sex. Fat is certainly part of how I came to feel like this—feeling unwanted, unwantable, and undesirable. But I think it comes from before fat. I think it comes from that one-year-old Woodman suggests I left behind. I think my bodily feelings got left behind with her. In a deep way, we daughters get our bodies from our mothers. My mother and her body had at best an uneasy relationship. For most of my life, she was or believed herself to be physically ill. Her body was an ongoing source of pain and disease for her. So how could she give me a positive connection to my own body?

When I think of myself as a little girl, I see me in a pink dress and I am twirling and trying to please Dad. See me. Want me. In photos of myself when Dad was the photographer, I see my face lit up for him. There is a photo of me at age one, the age Woodman says the soul goes underground. I am with my two brothers in the only photo of the three of us together. I am being held by my favorite brother and smiling at my beloved father. It was with my brother and my father and my grandmother that I felt loved and adored. But they could not give me what I needed from my mother.

I used to imagine that if I got thin, I would have to fend off attention from men, that somehow I would be devastatingly, dangerously attractive. When in college and a couple of times later I was pursued persistently by a man, I found fault in him as if there must be something wrong with him for being so eager to have me. When I was in Denver on my short-lived internship and at a low weight for me, I did attract a lot of attention. But rather than enjoy it, I found it almost unpleasant. When a man was interested in me, when he was the pursuer, I would back off. As much as I wanted to be wanted, when a man seemed to want me and I was not the initiator, I felt anxious. I just didn't trust that anyone who pursued me actually wanted me or was attracted to me. How could anyone who wanted me be worth becoming involved with? There was something compelling about trying to persuade, to charm, to seduce someone I wanted to want me. But then, even when I succeeded, I couldn't trust that it was real—because after all, I had made him want me. It was my Catch-22.

In 1973, Stockard Channing starred in a television movie, "The Girl Most Likely To …" In it, an ugly girl undergoes plastic surgery and becomes beautiful. She then takes revenge on all the people who mistreated her when she was ugly. I loved this movie because it made dark comedy of my own wish to punish the men, especially my husband, who made me feel unattractive and undesirable.

There was a tension between wanting to be the object of desire and huge anxiety when I was, and rage at men who made me feel undesirable. There was no just right position for me with men. I was always wanting and angry.

Men became both the people who have the power to make me feel I was lovable and who left me alone to deal with her. Always that tension. Always loving and hating. Wanting and rejecting. Tantalizing objects that I longed for.

> Woodman: *Once a woman is ready to break her identification with the mother, once consciousness understands what has been going on unconsciously, she can understand that her real mother, and therefore the mother within herself were simply not able to give food. So long as she is obedient to a mother—actual or internal—who unconsciously wishes to annihilate her, she is in a state of possession by the witch; she will have to differentiate herself out from that witch in order to live her own life.* (Woodman, 1990, p. 2)

I used to carry my anger with my mother all the time. She was my favorite target. Now sometimes when I think of her, I feel sad. Sad for her, because I know her life was not what she hoped for, sad for me because we never managed to connect in the way I wished. I can feel for her and what it was like to live for sixty-two years with a man who was unfaithful again and again starting the second year of their marriage and continuing to the end. Her entire adult life spent with him. Sixty-two years and they had maybe ten happy days, if that. That makes me sad. She was smart and I know had she been born when I was, she would have had so many more opportunities to explore her interests and do something. I want to believe she would have. She had wanted to go to nursing school when she graduated from high school in 1932.

But schools of nursing required that students not enroll before they turned eighteen and she was too young and her father denied her the needed permission to enter at seventeen. That same year she married my father, mostly to get away from her father who was strict and hard on her. And the next year she had her first baby. She never lived on her own, not really. Never had a place to herself, a room of her own. She went from being her father's daughter to being my father's wife. I wonder if she knew what she wanted or if she squelched all of that.

I remember when I was little seeing a picture of her with a man who had a parrot. I didn't know who the man was but I remember she was smiling and looked happy. One of my brothers believes he was a man she had an affair with while my father was away during the War. Those two years were very different for her. She worked in the co-op, starting as a cashier and ending as manager. That was the only time in her life that she had a job. They believe, and I want to believe also, because I want to believe that she did reach for something better for herself, we believe that she planned to leave my father and be with the man with the parrot.

My mother was the most asexual person I have ever known. I think it is not just the usual reluctance of children to see their parents as sexual beings that leads to all three of us seeing her as just not sexual at all. I hope she was in love with this other man, that she enjoyed him and being with him. I want for her to have had that. Once, I would have sneered at the idea that she could love anyone, but now, I want for her to have loved and been loved. My father returned home in September of 1945. I was born in July 1946. If what we believe is true, I dashed her hopes of being with this other man. Maybe that is why she was so unhappy and so angry with me. I can understand that.

She was very unhappy. My birth ushered in a long period of near invalidism for her. It is impossible now to know how much of what she suffered was due to actual illness and how much to somatising of her unhappiness, depression, and anger. She was hospitalized several times for illnesses of one kind or another and had surgery twice before I was four. There was no way for her to give to me what I, what any child needed. Her own needs were massive and unmet. She had nothing left to give to me. Except her anger and disappointment. Just as she was the target for me, I was hers. She was never toward my brothers as she was with me; they had a great deal of difficulty understanding my experiences with her when I did tell them because she was so different with them. Knowing that difference made it even harder for me. My grandmother told stories about when my brothers were growing up; as she described the family, it was very different from what I knew. And there are photos also where a much happier version of my mother held my brothers or was shown laughing. I didn't know that version of her; knowing she existed or had existed made my yearning greater.

She writes in that baby book about me that she was not able to breast-feed me as she had my brothers. It is unclear why, though I suspect it had to do with her medical problems following my birth and probably also represents her rejection of me. Thinking about that now, I wonder if that is why she fretted so about feeding me, about my eating—because she was unable to feed me herself. That failure, the literal inability to breastfeed me became a broader inability to feed me at all emotionally. It is as if something caused the milk she might have fed me to become toxic and poison us both.

As I have written about her, my compassion for her has deepened. And I have been able to see more how life with her actually was. I can see her wish that I not exist and mine that I punish her for not wanting and loving me. Mothering my own children went a long way toward healing some of these wounds. I am proudest in my life that I have been able to be a much better mother than I had and that my children have never had to ask if I loved them. Being with them as I so wanted my mother to be with me is terribly important to me.

So I am able to feel and accept and know that my "real mother, and therefore the mother within [myself] were simply not able to give food." I don't have to be angry with her anymore. But the second part, about being "obedient to a mother—actual or internal—who uncon-sciously wishes to annihilate her" is slower coming. The legacy of hav-ing actually been obedient to her is persistent. I grew up feeling that I am the mistake she said I was. It never occurred to me until a few years ago that the mistake was hers; it is not me or mine. My fat ampli-fied that feeling of not belonging, of having no place. My breath still catches when I let in the reality that at least unconsciously she wished to annihilate me.

After all this I was still not able to truly see how my mother's attitude toward me factored into my fat and then I read an interview with Marion Woodman, "Confronting the death mother." Somehow in this interview she managed not to fall into the clouds of images and metaphors she so frequently writes. In this interview she speaks clearly.

If, while growing up, we sensed that we were unacceptable to our parents, if we were not wanted, or if we intuited that we threatened our parents, then our nervous system will have become hyper-vigilant. Our cells will have been imprinted with a profound fear of abandonment; as a consequence our body will numb-out the moment that we feel threatened. As soon as we realize that we are no longer pleasing somebody, we freeze; we are thrown back into our belief that we are unlovable, which then activates our ever-present, but unconscious, terror of annihilation. In such moments the autonomic nervous system says "NO" and the ego withdraws. I call this being catapulted into "possum mentality"; as soon as we sense a whiff of rejection we are paralyzed with fear, we close down and we stay absolutely still in order to survive. Eventually, that possum becomes a permanent feature in our body-psyche; then life is experienced as a minefield in which we are knocked down by explosions that are inaudible to others. If there is unconscious hostility in the environment, the inner body, acting autonomously, retreats and falls over "dead". At the same time we may develop defense mechanisms that manifest in an armor of fat, oedema, vomiting, anything to keep poison out. Ultimately, our body may turn against itself as it does with cancer or auto-immune diseases. Death Mother has been incorporated into the fabric of our cells. (Sieff, 2009, p. 178)

In that paragraph, where she says "we may develop defense mecha-nisms ... to keep the poison out," right there I changed. I can feel my body as a defense against her in a way I couldn't when I began this journey, my body as a physical manifestation of my complex. The girl who became the woman who kept wishing and hoping that she could be close to her mother wants to shake her head and deny that, but I cannot. My fat arises in part from it—I have to be big in order to take up space, to assert my right to exist, to keep the poison out. Because underneath it all, in my obedience to her, I have believed I had no right to exist at all. I feel it in my shame about needing and in the struggle to accept myself as I am, in the flesh of the body that I inhabit.

In the end, looking at my mother complex as it relates to my weight is interesting certainly and I can see how the various and sundry physiolog-ical dispositions to becoming fat could and most likely did interact with my history and relationship with my mother. And understanding these things is valuable in understanding how I came to be the person I am. But it does not change anything really. It is still the case that height and weight are heritable to roughly the same degree; that weight is distributed normally like height is, so that it is expectable that there will be some people at either end of the distribution of weight. That does not mark them as pathological, merely as one or more standard deviations away from the norm. Furthermore, seeing where complexes and this physical characteristic interact does not make weight disappear, does not move me or any fat person to the center of that bell shaped curve and average. So the really important questions do not center around what makes one person fat and another slender, but rather what is the impact of being fat? How does being fat affect a person's life experience? Her self-perception? Her happiness and wellbeing? What, in other words, does it mean to be fat in a world that is hostile to fat? And Woodman does not have much to say about that, does not have much to offer to me or other fat women about how to live our lives, what being different in the ways that we are means for us and how best to respond to that. Only in that interview about the Death Mother from 2009 reflecting thinking that came about thirty years after her books about weight, does she begin to show understanding that there is something more at work than complexes. She hints at recognizing that trauma is involved here, something I will explore in a later chapter.

CHAPTER SIX

Woodman and anger, food, eating, and control

Woodman deals with issues around anger, food, and eating as complexes in themselves. I am not sure that I believe they are significantly different for fat people than for average or slender people. But I would be remiss if I did not also engage them as they are very much a part of beliefs in the larger culture about how fat comes about. It is in these areas that she is most a part of mainstream thinking about fat. I quote Woodman but her words could equally well have been written or said by many people writing about obesity and eating behavior.

Anger

Woodman: *They [the obese] have no sense of everlasting arms to uphold them through the crises of life; the early matrix with the mother isn't there. That deprivation propels them to make violent attempts to hold onto life; momentarily they may do so, and then sink back into a lethargy of nonexistence. Their existence is precarious at best because they have no sense of a daily continuum. Such girls may seek husbands who will provide that loving day-to-day cherishing, and therefore in marriage they*

may lock themselves yet again into the mother they sought to escape.
(Woodman, 1982, p. 21)

I hate considering that my rage and anger became my fat. It makes me feel guilty. It makes me feel that it *is* all my fault, that if I had been more conscious, less angry, I would have been slender. It makes me feel that my mother was right about me. It makes me feel sick to consider that her assertions about me became self-fulfilling prophecies that I have fulfilled. But I have to allow that it played some part in how my body came to be as it is.

> **Woodman:** *Unless she recognizes that her father-lover is her own inner ideal man who must not be projected onto a human man, she may spend her life searching for her ghostly lover. If she finds her "ideal", she may be bound for double-edged tragedy because the golden arrows will probably strike a puer searching for a mother. Their marriage would then be double incest.* (Woodman, 1980, p. 92)

So here we go—about my first marriage. There were lots of problems in my marriage starting with the painful reality that we wanted to be married more than we wanted to be married to each other, that we wanted a family more than we wanted each other. It is still hard for me to know if we were ever really in love. But we did marry. We built a joint psychotherapy practice together. We had and successfully parented two children together. We traveled together. We liked movies and eating out and laughing and exposing our children to art and music and other cultures. I suppose in most ways we were good friends. But there was always something missing and over time that missing element eroded the entire relationship.

From the time we got married until the time of the divorce, he kept telling me he would really love me when I weighed 120 pounds. Over the first ten years I went to Jazzercise, and Weight Watchers, tried Diet Workshop. I went to my doctor, who said he had experience helping people lose weight. I wrote down everything I ate. I dreamt about food. I got up in the morning thinking already about what I could have for dinner. I weighed myself every day. I made a chart, a graph to show my weight loss. That chart I made showed I was losing weight even though in reality I was gaining. The chart lied. I lied. He never noticed. He was still saying he would really love me when I weighed 120. I was making myself go further and further away from being really loved.

I was angry that he kept telling me throughout the marriage that he would really love me when I weighed 120 pounds, and he was angry that I never attained that goal. He betrayed me in the way that mattered most to me. I betrayed him in the way that mattered most to him. In a mostly silent battle we slowly annihilated whatever good feeling had kept us together. Anger was the strongest thing we had in common other than our children. I remember sitting across from him at lunch in a neighborhood restaurant and hearing him coolly and dispassionately tell me he just didn't find me attractive and I can feel the humiliation and anger I felt then.

In the twenty-four years we were married I gained 100 pounds. It wasn't from the food I ate. It was the anger I swallowed. The humiliation I accepted. Or was it?

> **Woodman:** *Helpless rage is rarely expressed by obese women … Their unexpressed feelings live in the cage of their compulsive drives waiting to burst out.* (Woodman, 1980, p. 32)

If I had left him at the beginning, would I be like the girl in photos of me from 1970, not long before I married, would I be an older version of her? Would I be 100 pounds thinner? I recoil at the thought. Did I do that to myself? I cannot possibly know what would have happened had I not been so angry with him all those years. If I had left, way back in Connecticut that first time he said it was too bad he wasn't in love with me, if I had believed that there would be someone who would fall in love with me and I with him … I groan at the thought. It might have been that I married and had children with a man who wanted me, wanted the life I wanted, who cherished what we had and shaped together, like I have now. What would it be like to have children born of that kind of relationship? What would it be like to have developed my career, friendships, a life in that kind of relationship? I literally ache, I hurt when I imagine this, that I might have had something so very different. I feel sick with the thought that I did it to myself. And it cannot be undone.

I can look at what happened, see that I gained those pounds over those years that I was so angry, and I could, as Marion Woodman would have me do, conclude that there is causation there. But I resist it.

Correlation after all is not causation. I don't want it all to be my fault, something I could have prevented. Because the pain of that is so big. That I stayed with him, that I married him is bad enough. But not only could I have been considerably thinner, I could have had a very different life had I not been so afraid of being alone—that is almost unbearable to consider. Staying with that renders me awash in grief and regret at what I did to my life. I can tell myself that what I did was what I had to do to have what I have, the love I have now, but it sounds too pat, too Pollyannaish. No matter that I have a better life now, have a husband who truly loves me and whom I love, have two children who in many ways are the best of their parents, still I destroyed something important when I agreed to make a life with a man who wouldn't love me and whom I came to hate. That life is better now does not compensate for that loss. I arrive at knowing something I can hardly bear to let in, that I abandoned my own life for a man who did not want me. My desperation to be wanted blinded me to reality. It makes me cry and want to hide, feel ashamed and full of rage at myself. It makes me feel that this body is what I must wear as the emblem of my disregard of myself, for having been with him all those years. My body reveals my rage and hatred for my mother, my terrible unmet need for her, for my father for not defending me and now the rage I swallowed to be married to a man who did not want me. Yes, and I see I fall into the trap of thinking that somehow I would be better if I were thinner.

Anger at my mother, anger at my father, at my husband, at the blind date who called me a dog. I was very angry. But expressing that anger has always been difficult. I thought that because I fought with her so much and so often, that I was expressing my anger to my mother. But what I was expressing was defiance. My anger came out in knowing I could always get the last word, that I could hurt her with my words. I was afraid to be direct and open with my anger, to tell her how I felt about her threats and irrationality. My anger congealed into contempt. That I shouted at her never got close to the helpless rage at her I felt. To openly express my rage at her, my father, my husband, anyone, the thought of doing that makes me anxious and I am gripped by the fear that I will be abandoned, rejected, made to feel even worse than the worst I have ever felt, that I will be annihilated, erased. So it comes out feebly in sarcasm or disguised as humor, or sometimes in tears that look like sadness. But in finding direct and open expression of anger difficult am I really different from most women of my time and culture?

Are we not still writing about the need for women to find our voices and express our anger? That is not about fat; it is about being a woman in a culture that does not endorse strong negative expression from women, expression of emotion or ideas that make others, especially men uncomfortable.

It is true that in the twenty-six years that I was in a relationship with my first husband, I gained 100 pounds, and some would attribute that weight gain to swallowed anger. Sometimes I do that. But it is also true that in that time, I dieted and lost thirty pounds or more three times and each time I regained all the weight I lost plus more so that by the time I stopped dieting I weighed more than I had when I started. And in that time, I bore two children. In each of those pregnancies I gained less than twenty-five pounds. But after each, instead of losing the pregnancy weight, despite my efforts to the contrary, I lost none of it. So after two pregnancies, I was nearly fifty pounds heavier than I was before. This is not about swallowed anger. As Dr. Arya Sharma has written:

> Rather than a simple lack of willpower, the relapse of most indi-
> viduals to their previous weight after otherwise successful weight
> loss is largely driven by the coordinated actions of metabolic, neu-
> roendocrine, autonomic, and behavioural changes that oppose the
> maintenance of reduced body weight. (Sharma, 2014)

And in those twenty-six years, the women's movement came to life. Most of the women I knew were angry. Angry about gender discrimination. Angry about men. Angry about inequality. There was a lot of anger among women then. I was angry too. The very first issue of *Ms* magazine came out the month after I married. I was a charter subscriber.

Food and eating

Woodman: *The obese and the anorexic are fighting their battles for con-*
sciousness through food—the acceptance or rejection of it. (Woodman,
1980, p. 20)

Initially, I can't respond to this. I have the feeling that anything I might say appears defensive. How many times must I, or people like me, say that food is not the issue, not for all of us? Austin, Ogden, and Hill in their work reveal that while everyone is eating more calories now than they were back in 1971, "naturally" thin people somehow manage to stay thin, while "calorie-sensitive" people get heavier (Austin, Ogden, & Hill, 2011). Thus, the laws of physics which would tell us that fat people gain weight because they simply eat more and move less don't quite tell us why thin people can eat more and move less and still stay thin.

I know Woodman isn't saying what I am hearing. And I know that somewhere in what I can't hear is something important for me to understand. But I can't hear it because I don't binge and I don't eat compulsively. I know it seems impossible to anyone who is not fat that actually I eat the way most of them do. Intuitively that makes no sense. I know that. Some time ago when I first began to present some of this material, I encountered this problem. I was asked on several occasions about what I do eat because my questioner had difficulty understanding how it could be that I do not eat significantly differently from the way she did. How do I respond when the question reflects the belief, so common in our culture, that I am fat because of the way I eat, that if I ate as they do, I would be thin too? And why should I respond? The very fact that I feel I must defend how and what I eat comes from a lifetime of battling with these stereotypes. But in defending, I am also buying into the validity of their assumptions just as when I try to find the cause, any cause for my fat I am tacitly accepting the underlying assumption that fat is wrong, bad or pathological—anything but normal. I need to find for myself what is true and relevant for me, without feeling I must apologize for my size or believe myself to be "disordered."

Woodman: *Food becomes the focus for depression, for repressed anger, for anxiety, for repressed sexuality.* (Woodman, 1980, p. 20)

When all we hear is about the potential danger in food—all the worry about fat, sugar, calories, and eating—how can food not become something other than nourishment? It is so difficult for food to be just food. Though I know I eat moderately and healthily—whatever that is—I am self-conscious much of the time when I eat with people I do not know well. I become self-conscious because of what I believe people believe about me and eating based on what people have said to me and what I have heard them say of others. So, for example, I almost never order dessert when I am out with people other than my family or very close friends. Eating places me in the panopticon.

Eating, not eating, dieting, good foods, bad foods, healthy foods, junk foods—we spend so much of our lives wrestling with this business of nourishing ourselves.

I remember when I was a teenager and I would root through the kitchens of the people I babysat for and look for things to eat. Things I would not ordinarily eat. Like raw Jell-O. It was forbidden. I always ate things and then worried that they would be discovered missing. And I snooped and looked at photos and read letters. I was devouring the details of their lives. In *Fat Girl* Judith Moore tells of breaking into her minister's house again and again and lying on their bed and eating their food, sneaking there to take what she wanted. She says,

> You who are reading here may have an idea about why I lolled around June's apartment and ate her canned goods and about why I broke into the Fisher's ranch-style house and rather dangerously hung around and made afternoon snacks. I was hungry for love. I know that. But so are many sad and hungry children and they don't rummage people's living quarters and eat their food. (Moore, 2005, p. 174)

Why is this so hard to acknowledge? I have never talked with anyone about it. I feel a combination of shame and denial because I recognize in me the same desperate for love girl that Judith Moore writes of so fearlessly.

A vivid memory I have of college is eating a type of really large soft oatmeal sandwich cookie that was way too sweet but which I know I ate when I was unhappy and feeling out of the social swing of things. I used to go to the Duke East Campus Dope Shop—and how oddly appropriate that name was—to get one and sit and eat it and drink my large Tab, alone and feeling sorry for myself.

Or making peanut butter fudge when my parents were out and eating it before they came home. Another fudge memory from when I was around four—my mother is on the telephone talking with a friend of hers and I run in and out of the room taking each time a piece of peanut butter fudge from the candy jar on the table until there was hardly any left. Sneaking something from her while she wasn't looking. Something sweet.

There was an element of defiance to it all then. I see that. I feel that. I hate talking about it. I hate talking about it because it fits so well into the dominant narrative about how and what fat people eat. When I stopped dieting, when I stopped fighting with my body, something remarkable happened—my relationship with food changed. When I stopped dieting about thirty-five years ago, I ended the whole good foods/bad foods thing, so much a part of dieting. Dieting requires that the universe of foods be divided into good and bad, virtuous and sinful. When I stopped dieting, those categories ended and so did eating as defiance.

I read a book challenging dieting many years ago so the title is lost to me now. What I remember most from it is a very common-sense exchange between the author and a woman who says she is returning to Weight Watchers. The author asks her how many times she has done that program before. The woman says this will be her fourth time. And the author asks her what she will learn this time that is new? Indeed every time someone returns to Weight Watchers they go expecting that this time it will work, this time they will reach goal weight and stay there. This time they will find the pot of gold at the end of the rainbow, that the elusive magic will appear. Only hardly anyone ever succeeds long term. The business model of these weight loss programs depends on a high "relapse" rate with members returning multiple times. When I first went to Weight Watchers—and I did that program three times—I was given a goal weight of 127. In those days receiving a goal weight was part of beginning the program and somehow that goal carried a kind of authority. I have no idea really how that figure was derived. I suspect it was from some version of the Metropolitan Life weight tables with the invented notion of frame size and use of faulty actuarial data. The last time I weighed 127 was sometime in my early teens. There was no way I was going to achieve that goal, no matter how hard I tried. But somehow I was supposed to believe that 127 was the magic point at which I would be right, I would be okay, I would be normal. And anything more than that, any weight higher was a mark against me, an indicator of my failure, my weakness, my inability to tame my wayward appetite. Weight Watchers and my husband both wanting me to become a weight I never achieved.

When I stopped dieting, it scared me at first to try allowing myself to eat what I wanted when I was hungry, not what was "legal" or "good" or even "healthy" but what I wanted. And eat until I had had enough. I was afraid when I contemplated doing that because I was certain my weight would balloon up to 400 pounds or more. That was what I was

supposed to be afraid of, what the dieting made me believe. I was supposed to believe that unless held in check through a diet, my appetite
would run amok and I would have no control at all. I believed it was
only by rigid control, by keeping my finger in the dike of my hunger
that I could keep from becoming monstrously fat. A line heard recently
in a movie—a slender woman rejects a doughnut offered to her, saying,
"I love them but I never eat them or I would soon look like one." I feared
that but it didn't happen. Along the way, I discovered that I don't really
like sweet things all that much—I could never eat one of those oatmeal
sandwich cookies now—and that many times a salad is more desirable
than dessert. It was only through the process of allowing myself to eat
what and when I wanted and to stop when I had had enough, only
through eliminating bad and good as categories, that I learned that I
like sour and salty, dislike bitter and am not all that interested in sweet
tastes. Dieting never allowed me to even know what I liked because a
diet does not trust the eater to know such things.

I never binged. I don't know what it is to eat myself into oblivion.
I never got up in the middle of the night to eat, never raided the
refrigerator in the night. Or loaded up on mountains of doughnuts and
things to eat until I passed out or felt so full I was sick. I never did
that. Thus I have never thought of myself as a compulsive eater. My
eating did not fit what I knew about it as a disorder. Time to take a
closer look.

A definition of compulsive eating:

> an eating disorder characterized by continuous or frequent exces-
> sive eating over which an individual does not feel he or she has
> control, and which usually leads to weight gain and obesity. Eating
> is not connected to hunger, and food intake may be rapid or secret.
> Compensatory behaviors like purging, laxative use, or excessive
> exercise do not occur. Generally the amount eaten at any one time
> is not large; when it is, the disorder is usually called binge eating.
> (Mosby's Medical Dictionary, n.d.)

That could have been me. It is true I never binged but I was a compulsive eater according to this definition. My face gets hot because when
I was younger, especially when I was a teenager, this was true of me:
"Eating is not connected to hunger, and food intake may be rapid or
secret." I feel a rush of shame. Why shame? Because it means I was,

I am one of "those" people and I was out of control. Or was I? Samantha Murray raises this same question:

> ... the question is this: can a fat woman eat anything without being seen as addicted to food? Can a fat woman be regarded as not being out of control around food? Can a fat woman simply be hungry? While her food intake may be modest even by "healthy" standards, the fact that she is eating at all becomes a reinforcement of the perception of the fat body's constant indulgence of its (allegedly) excessive desires. (Murray, 2009, p. 44)

Eating is always problematic for a fat woman, no matter how or what she eats. Because if she is seen eating at all, others believe she is giving evidence of what they believe about her.

The biggest problem I have with Woodman is her persistent insistence that fat people are compulsive eaters. It is infuriating to deal with that assumption, which seems to be the most commonly held one about fat people, when I know I don't eat that way, and if I don't, I know there are other fat people who also do not. Yet any effort I make to protest the assumption then becomes evidence of my denial.

> **Woodman:** *The need for love is ... easily confused with the need for food. Since love is so much a part of life, tasting food is tasting life ...* (Woodman, 1980, p. 21)

Of course tasting food is tasting life. We celebrate with food. Holidays have special foods at their center. The Church calendar is full of feast days. Special foods when we feel sick, and yes, food is sometimes substituted for love. I have no arguments to mount. But I do not think that food is the issue or the obsession, unless one is dieting. It is the hunger for love and being wanted that becomes obsessive. There need be no confusion of food and love for this to happen. But wait. Tasting food *is* tasting life, one of the sensual pleasures of life. Is it only problematic when fat people enjoy it?

I love to cook. I love to prepare good meals for friends and family. I love to eat good food. But if I talk too easily of food and of my love of it, I run the risk of drawing judgment. I can see in the glances exchanged, the words not spoken: the belief that I am fat because I eat too much, because I take too much pleasure in food. But I am not obsessed with food. I was when I dieted—all dieters are. Carol Bloom agrees:

> Eating or restricting food without reference to hunger and satiation, berating oneself for eating, and for needing to eat, being obsessively concerned about food, and devaluing one's body are the common characteristics of all eating problems. Body insecurity leads to dieting which leads to bingeing (mentally and/or behaviorally), which leads to further starving, purging, dieting or overexercising in an endless cycle. These dynamics apply to women in hospitals on the verge of death, to "ordinary" women who diet several times a year, and to all who never diet but declare their need to do so many times a day. (Bloom, 1994, p. xii)

The obsession is a function of dieting. Surely this kind of obsession is what Woodman describes as compulsive. Food obsession is the name of the game when you diet. Good foods, bad foods, legal foods. Weighing and measuring foods. Counting calories or points or fat grams or carb grams. The focus all day every day is on what can and can't be eaten and feelings of shame and guilt at any lapse, at any tasting of forbidden fruit. Recording every morsel eaten with greater attention than to the most enthusiastically kept journal. I don't do that now that I am not dieting. It took a long time for me to learn that I can eat what I want when I want it and stop when I have had enough, which means I don't have to think about food all the time.

I also love to read, knit, smell flowers, look at paintings, and touch things. The sound of words, of music, the tactile experience of silk, cashmere, and wool yarns slipping through my fingers, the vibrancy of color. I have great sensory appetite for those things.

> **Woodman:** *The death wish in the heart of the primarily obese is not to be overlooked. It is the other side of a fierce desire for life, for sexuality, for all the Dionysian passion for which their powerful bodies have fitted them, but which life in this society has denied them.* (Woodman, 1980, p. 57)

In this place, Woodman seems to be saying that it is the condemnation by society, the cultural phobia about fat that keeps that fierce desire for life and passion from finding expression except in the large body itself.

I sigh. Where I can feel powerless is in the face of condemning judgments of me and my body that I encounter every day. I can't stop them. I remember the humiliation I felt when a waiter asked if I really needed the dessert I ordered. Humiliation and rage that I don't express. I know the judgments are there. I want to be immune to them.

Control

When I was dieting and wanting more than anything to lose weight, to be normal, and the weight would stop coming off or I would see the pounds coming back, I would fall into despair. It all seemed so hopeless. No matter how hard I tried, no matter how little I ate, I couldn't get my body to comply. I was ashamed. I felt ugly. I felt like a failure. I felt it must be my fault. My powerlessness was not in the face of the obsession, or not obsession with food. It was the obsession with becoming thin that gripped me and I was powerless to bend my body to my will.

> **Woodman**: *The obese adolescent who diets becomes discouraged, binges and starves without becoming thin, and learns to experience herself as an ugly, cowardly failure in the eyes of her parents and peer group.* (Woodman, 1980, p. 57)

That feeling of being ugly and a failure doesn't spring up in isolation. Fat children and teens are told over and over again directly and indirectly that they are not acceptable. And fat women hear those same messages also. All those years of dieting, and dealing with "friends" who decided to make me a project and tell me what to eat and where and when. Everywhere I look is a message that I am too much, take up too much space, should be taxed, starved, punished. When I run across comments like the following, left on a news article about there being five percent more overweight people than hungry people in the world, I am angry but I also feel a visceral fear and sense of being outside, other, alien:

> Cut slabs of meat off the fat people, and feed it to the skinny people.
> When things get really bad, a starving person should be allowed to eat one obese person per year.

Ultimate Robin Hood: Liposuction the fat to feed the skinny.

So, harvest the fatties; ship them to the Third World; and sell them as "horse" meat.

Oh good. The potential food supply (fatties) now outnumbers the hungry.

Let the hungry people eat the obese people. Problem solved! (Big liberty, 2011)

It is not only that fat-hating comments appears in the comments section of news articles, but there are also whole groups devoted to fat hating, where members, posting anonymously, can go vent their hatred.

> A few months ago, Reddit made news because it banned a 150,000-strong group dedicated to tracking down and harassing fat people (don't worry, several fat-hating subreddits are still there, at least one with over 100,000 members). The existence of those groups surprised some people—not that there was mockery of the overweight, but that there was frothing, pathological hatred of them. And if you're an overweight female, then God help you—girls' self-esteem is inversely proportional to their body weight. And this is because society makes it clear that the overweight are inhuman, soulless monsters. (Fitzgerald, 2015)

More than 100,000 people who want to post hatefully about fat and fat people on a regular basis. Try to imagine what it is like knowing that there are people out there who do that for fun. How do I deal with knowing that these feelings are out there? That likely any time I go out, someone sees me with those kinds of eyes?

I read this in a blog on Medscape, which deals with medical news and opinion:

> "If physicians want to decrease their risk in managing patients by excluding obese patients who are at higher risk for complications," he writes. "Shouldn't they be able to do so? … The more that physicians who care for higher-risk patients are sued for less than perfect outcomes, the less that those physicians will be willing to treat higher-risk patients."

> This stance has generated a lot of heated comments, but many doctors feel this way, especially in our adversarial malpractice climate. Until that changes, I would expect more physicians to be wary of taking patients prone to medical complications. (Pho, 2011)

It isn't bad enough to have to deal with doctors who see fat rather than a patient, but now they want to be able to refuse to treat me, even in an emergency room, and I am to believe this is because of some unproven risk. It was only in June of 2014 that the American College of Obstetricians and Gynecologists felt moved to issue ethical guidelines on treating fat patients. The guidelines are:

- Physicians should be prepared to care for obese patients in a nonjudgmental manner, being cognizant of the medical, social, and ethical implications of obesity.
- Recommendations for weight loss should be based on medical considerations.
- An understanding that weight loss entails more than simply counseling a woman to eat less and exercise more and a willingness to learn about the particular causes of a patient's obesity will assist physicians and other health care professionals working with them in providing effective care.
- Physicians can serve as advocates within their clinical settings for the necessary resources to provide the best possible care to obese women.
- *It is unethical for physicians to refuse to accept a patient or decline to continue care that is within their scope of practice solely because the patient is obese.* However, if physicians lack the resources necessary for the safe and effective care of the obese patient, consultation or referral or both are appropriate.
- Physicians should work to avoid bias in counseling regardless of their own body mass index status.
- Obesity education that focuses on the specific medical, cultural, and social issues of the obese woman should be incorporated into physician education at all levels. (ACOG, 2014) [Emphasis added]

It boggles my mind that in a profession with an oath that includes "First do no harm" even needs to have a statement like the one I made italicized above.

Is what Woodman sees as a death wish inherent in fat all there is to that wish? Or does it also arise in response to a culture in which I know myself to be seen as not fully human, as not worthy of the same care as slender people? Start with a rejecting mother, add huge doses of societal rejection and how likely is it there wouldn't be a death wish, however submerged it may be?

I have enjoyed reading much of Sam Keen's writing. But here he writes the thoughts that I am sometimes afraid others are thinking:

> I was just coming out of the men's room in the San Francisco airport when she waddled toward me. Her two hundred and fifty plus pounds was distributed over her short frame in way that made her appear nearly round, but her loosely draped, dappled paisley silk lent a hint of elegance to her movement. All by herself she was a parade of mammoth and grotesque proportions.
>
> As she approached nearer I could see that her eyes were focused on something just in back of me. I turned to see a slim, classically handsome airline pilot, the man of her dreams, for a moment at least. Turning back I saw in her eyes a reflected image of a couple–the pilot and the slim woman she was a long time ago and is still in the sanctuary of her imagination.
>
> What happened to cause her to hide her loveliness, her dream, within the impenetrable mountain of her flesh? What pain? What betrayal? What disappointment? What lost love left her so hungry? (Keen, 2015, n.d.)

Is it so unimaginable to him, to most thin people, that she has love of her own, that someone loves her as she is? Keen sees her as mammoth and grotesque but that doesn't mean everyone does, that a handsome airline pilot is not waiting for her at home. But most people will see her as Keen does. I know this and I feel it.

And I feel ambivalent. Fat acceptance is one thing. Being happy in my body as it is is another. I am ambivalent about my body. About what any of this means. About all of it. I am not sure where the line is between resignation and acceptance. How could I not be ambivalent? I have learned to stop hating my fat body. That took a long time. I accept that this is my body. I no longer try to starve my body into submission and become some other more socially acceptable version of myself. But do I love the fat arms I glimpse when I walk by a mirror? Or the roll of fat above my waist? Or my big belly and thighs? I don't hate them, but I cannot say I love them either. Furthermore, I know I am in good company because it is very difficult to find any woman, regardless of her weight, who is entirely happy with her body. At least I have made peace with mine. That may be as good as it gets. Or it is for now.

> **Woodman:** *Since love is so much a part of life, tasting food is tasting life, but conversely, avoiding food may be avoiding life. The system of punishment and reward in relation to feeding the obese body becomes a moral issue. When they feel rejected by others, they tend to compensate for their loss by eating; when they are angry with themselves, they punish their bodies by eating; when they are happy, they reward their bodies by not eating.* (Woodman, 1980, p. 21)

No one ever asked me if this is how it is for me. Most people seem to assume that I eat too much or eat in some way different from the way thin people eat, different from the way they themselves eat and that it is a taboo topic. But look at what Woodman states as a given. What support does she have? Does she know that this behavior is common for people who have dieted a lot, no matter their weight? This behavior that she describes, that food becomes the center of everything, is part and parcel of dieting and having to work and spend a great deal of energy on trying to control the body. It is not particular to fat people or to anorexics. For anyone dieting, food becomes love or comfort or reward. Is it at all likely that all of the people who have decided they are gluten intolerant actually are or what their obsession means? There is a word for this preoccupation with food that anyone who has dieted experiences, which many people in our current anti-fat and health obsessed culture experience daily: orthorexia, an obsession with eating only foods that one considers healthy.

I seize on Woodman's statement, I know, because it contains so much assumption. When I can become self-righteously angry, I can more easily reject what she says. The truth in what she says is that I have a huge need for love. But I don't try to satisfy it with food. Not now. Not in my life today. And yes, I do know that what is true for me is not true for everyone. Indeed there are fat people who eat as she described and thin people who do the same.

I can see what she says about dieting, and about bingeing. I can also see it sometimes when I am under a lot of stress. But my reaction to being depressed or upset is to not eat, not turn to food. Dieters, or restrained eaters, eat when depressed. But non-dieters, fat or thin, report loss of appetite with depression as Herman and Polivy (1980) found. Woodman's assertion is an example of a generalization that just is not supported. I am bothered by the equation she makes between obesity and compulsive eating. I know that eating compulsively is a behavior that many people employ quite often, both fat and thin people. And it is not clear to me that as a behavior, it is enough to be considered a disorder. Just as I find it difficult to agree with Woodman that obesity, like anorexia, is a disorder. Obesity is a physical characteristic, anorexia a psychiatric disorder. One is based solely on weight and appearance, the other a collection of signs and symptoms. Furthermore, is it not true for many women who are not fat that they eat compulsively? Look at the scenes in movies and books and talk among women about eating a pint or more of ice cream to console themselves over some slight, loss, or upset. I know a normal weight woman who compulsively eats several tablespoons of peanut butter every night even as she condemns herself for doing so. Is it only problematic when fat women do it? My analyst says "Women become fat by doing it—as you did." And I want to scream at him—NO NO NO! Every woman I know does this and not every one of them becomes fat. Every body does not react the same way to food. The culprit is not food. It is something else, something more— the hunger? And a disposition to gain weight. But it exists even when food has ceased to be the focus it once was. Murray tells us that:

> Helen Keane compellingly interrogates the conflation of obesity and compulsive overeating, asserting that: Those who remain thin despite eating much more than others are more likely to be considered lucky than viewed as suffering from an eating disorder. And because they would not experience the intense conflict between appetite and the desire to lose weight which characterises the overweight overeater, they escape the feeling of being out of control which defines compulsion. Put simply, *it is only people who are trying to restrain their eating who experience it as compulsive.* (Murray, 2009) [Emphasis added]

Harry Guntrip (1969), a British psychoanalyst, said that people would rather be bad than weak, would rather believe that they are at fault for what is wrong than believe that they are powerless. Certainly this is at play for those who feel that they are fat because they eat too much, the wrong things, have too little control, and so forth. When I saw myself as weak-willed, slothful, an overeater, shameful in my excess, I certainly subscribed to the notion that I was bad, not weak. And if it is because I am bad, then if I work hard enough and become good, things will change, I will no longer be fat. Because to be weak is to accept that my body is not something I can force to be the way I want it to be. I had to keep trying to diet it into submission, somehow to make it be different.

> **Woodman:** *Dieting with fierce will-power is the masculine route; dieting with love is the feminine.* (Woodman, 1980, p. 100)

Woodman is half right. Trying to beat the body into submission is the masculine route, treating the body as an object that must be mastered, or as a wild thing that must be bent to a fierce will. But dieting with love is the same thing disguised with nicer words, the iron fist in a velvet glove. Because the vast majority of fat women will see diet after diet fail, no matter how lovingly undertaken as the body asserts its natural shape and the weight returns. Caring for my body, really caring for and about it means not dieting, not imposing rigid control over it. Is there any reason that my Self cannot be born of this fat vessel?

> **Woodman:** *To attempt to enforce strict discipline on an ego that has been raped all its life merely reinforces the psychology of the victim and with it the compensatory rebel and liar. Compulsive dieting reinforces already firmly entrenched compulsive patterns and releases more violent compensatory instinctual needs, creating a conflict which tears the soul to shreds and may lead to a psychotic break or suicide. So long as a woman secretly despises her own womanhood, fears her own sexuality, flagellates her body with curses and starvation or food that is poison to her, no healing can take place, however fat or thin she may become.* (Woodman, 1985, p. 107)

It seems almost radical for Woodman to say this, especially in light of the current focus on losing weight almost at any cost. Yet throughout her writing is the implicit assumption that doing the work in analysis will result in a new ability to lose weight. She never quite comes close to suggesting that one possible positive outcome would be to accept even a fat body as one's own and to delight in it but here she comes close.

Woodman: *Most of us can recognize what we call the negative mother archetype, the voice inside that asks, "Who do you think you are?" More difficult to endure is the death blow that swings out of the unconscious, paralyzing every cell of the body. The tension between trying and giving up becomes palpable. Ego tells the body to keep driving ahead; body tries to obey. The crux in this conflict may not become clear for months.*

A genuinely positive outcome requires a loving space, what I call a loving Presence that fills the molecules of the space around. It is a Presence that hears and loves the other as he/she is, a Presence that radiates from the depths of the unconscious with archetypal power (the life instinct), the only power strong enough to overcome the Death Mother. (Woodman, 2004)

What would this look like, to make space for this positive outcome? If not by dieting and beating the body into submission, how might that space be found, that space in which the Death Mother can be overcome?

Kim Chernin asks us to look at the fat woman differently, to see her with her "rounded cheeks, plump arms, ... broad shoulders, ... full thighs, rounded ass ... of a woman made that way according to her nature, walking with head high in pride of her body, however it happened to be shaped" (Chernin, 1994, p. 28). We need, she insists, to see each woman as she is meant to be, ripe and full of promise, not cut her down to some Procrustean ideal. That would be to care for her body lovingly, loving her exactly as she is.

And Clarissa Pinkola Estes offers:

> There is no "supposed to be" in bodies. The question is not size of or shape or years of age, or even having two of everything, for some do not. But the wild issue is, does this body feel, does it have right connection to pleasure, to heart, to soul, to the wild? Does it have happiness, joy? Can it in its own way move, dance, jiggle, sway, thrust? Nothing else matters. (Estes, 1992, p. 212)

For me this is what it means to care for my body, to respond to my body with love. And when I do, that wonderful fat woman with ribbons in her hair who came to me in a dream years ago dances and smiles and becomes real. Or I become in my mind's eye like one of the goddesses sculpted by Adam Schultz which can be seen on his website. Wonderful abundant bodies, women fully in their bodies, unashamed and exuberant.

CHAPTER SEVEN

A last look at Woodman

In her review of *The Owl was a Baker's Daughter*, Thelma Bryant summarizes Woodman. She begins: "Certainly not eating, as in anorexia nervosa, becomes a form of suicide and compulsive over-eating to the point of obesity may be considered another form of suicide, figurative if not literal" (Bryant, 1981, p. 27). I see again the equation of obesity with compulsive overeating and the comparison with anorexia. Anorexia is a disorder, an effort to escape the body, to rise above it; obesity is not. Obese is a body type. Not only that, but recent research finds: "The science around obesity does support the contention of so many people that in spite of a healthy diet and getting exercise, they continue to gain weight" (Sharma, 2011). In fact, one can be fat and anorexic. And what is this equation of becoming fat with a death wish as if being fat is a choice?

When I think about it, I feel angry and upset knowing that most people who see me believe that I am consciously responsible for my weight, unwilling to reign in gluttonous appetite. I want to yell, "IT'S NOT MY FAULT!" but what good would that do? Most doctors, thera-pists, and analysts would see me as resisting. The others would think I am just making excuses, refusing to take responsibility for myself. What makes the psychological pathologising of fat people particularly noxious is that although it is based on nothing but speculation, it is very difficult to refute. If I argue that fat is a physical characteristic, not a marker for psychopathology, I am being defensive. Indeed for those who believe it, denial seems only to support the case they have for pathologising fat people. It's a fat person's catch-22.

What of my normal weight friends who eat chocolate to make themselves feel better when they are upset or depressed? Or the whole notion of "comfort foods" which the term suggests food that serves as something other than a nutritional or social purpose? Is this okay for those who are not fat but indicative of psychopathology in fat people? As Rebecca Weinstein puts it in *Fat Kids*:

> ... eating is a way to be nurtured from the inside, and there is nothing wrong with that. The problem lies with the guilt a person feels after they eat the ice cream because they are lonely, and when it's gone they are still lonely. Many stop there, with the logic that ice cream does not solve loneliness. That is not the true key, however. It is not that eating ice cream and still feeling lonely is an offense. Eating ice cream may not cure loneliness, but it is still nurturing from the inside. The true dilemma is that guilt causes shame, and shame makes us feel not only lonely, but unlovable. The feeling of being unlovable is the true culprit, the catalyst in the cycle. (Weinstein, 2014, p. 39)

I have to accept and absorb that in coming to grips with my body, my fat, my life, it doesn't matter how my normal friends eat or what they do to comfort themselves. What matters for me is how I have used food to comfort myself, for other than nutritional or social purposes. Even then, it is not automatically cause for me to judge myself or see myself as broken somehow for doing so. And if comfort is traditionally linked with mother and mother with food, what is the problem exactly with "comfort food," except of course if it is the only form of comfort taken?

Then I wrestle with this "figurative suicide"—what is it? Statistically the suicide rate is lower in fat women. It has been suggested that the very hope which leads so many to believe that the next diet, the next means to banish fat will work and slenderness will be achieved at last, that very hope is what makes suicide rates lower, because hope mitigates against suicide. I know I am becoming too literal. I suppose that it could be argued that being fat is a kind of social suicide, rendering a person less socially desirable because fat does not conform to the social ideal. But suicide is a voluntary act and being fat, becoming fat is not. Am I again being too literal?

Or it is suggested that eating is a form of self-medication against despair. So what is this "figurative suicide"? The me who has died as a result of being fat is the me who tried so hard to believe that if only I could work this out, resolve these issues, then I would be thin. The me who is no longer, because she never existed, is the thin woman who people say lives inside a fat woman and screams to get out.

What I do know is that I no longer have the fantasy that I will become thin and that my life will all miraculously fall into place then. That fantasy died.

Where I see a figurative suicide is the death of vibrancy, color, and zest when I succumb to shame at the too-muchness of my body and I, in the face of my failure to shrink my body, shrink my life instead and retreat into a world where happiness is an ever elusive target entirely dependent on the judgment of the scales or how others see me. Where the fantasy of having a lithe body substitutes for celebrating in the body I have. Where the experience of being judged and the prejudice I encounter makes me afraid to venture out. I have done that, less now than when I was younger, but it is still there. Estes writes:

> Destroying a woman's instinctive affiliation with her natural body cheats her of confidence. It causes her to perseverate about whether she is a good person or not, and bases her self-worth on how she looks instead of who she is. It pressures her to use up her energy worrying about how much food she consumes or the readings on the scale or tape measure. It helps keep her preoccupied, colors everything she does, plans and anticipates. It is unthinkable in the instinctive world that a woman should live preoccupied by appearance this way. (Estes, 1992, p. 201)

Back to Bryant: "There seems to be a serious defect in the structure of the self in both the anorexic and the obese woman" (1981, p. 28). This makes me feel angry and hopeless because she states it so flatly and with such certainty. What do I with that?—I have a defect in the structure of my self? What does that mean for me? Do I have to become thin to fix it? Is it fixable? The anorexic starts to eat and gains weight and becomes normal or does she?—does that repair her self? Is it repairable? I am

supposed to simply accept this, that there is a serious defect in the structure of my self as indicated by my fat? or does my fat cause the defect?
And what is the defect in me? What on earth does that mean? And how
would I know? This statement sounds a lot like one of those "everybody
knows" statements about fat and fat people. It's like that former analyst
telling me that every extra ounce costs a pound of consciousness. I must
be approaching weightlessness in consciousness—and anorexics must
be more conscious than anyone. It makes no sense. It feels like another
way I am unacceptable, failed, flawed, and broken. The words make me
feel defensive right away. I have to fight my way through my defenses
to engage what she is saying. It seems to me that essentially what she is
saying is that to be fat is to be defective.

So what is the defect and how does one find it? Can it really be that
every fat person has this "serious defect in the structure of the self" and
how did it come to be attached to weight? How did weight, body size,
become a diagnostic marker for this defect? When other Jungians, other
therapists, read that, do they nod their heads sagely in agreement? Is
there a DSM V diagnosis for that defect? I have trouble not fixating
on what I see in this as not useful or helpful. I feel compelled to argue
with her. The dictionary tells us that a defect is a shortcoming, fault, or
flaw. A fault, a flaw, an imperfection. That is what Bryant says is in the
structure of the self of a fat person.

Is a fat body flawed just by virtue of being fat? Must a body be slender
in order to not show imperfection or a shortcoming? But not too slender
because she says that the anorexic also has this defect. This assumes
there is a perfect body, an ideal. According to Jung:

> If a woman strives for perfection she forgets the complementary
> role of completeness, which, though imperfect by itself, forms the
> necessary counterpart to perfection. For, just as completeness is
> always imperfect, so perfection is always incomplete, and therefore
> a final state which is hopelessly sterile … the imperfectum carries
> within it the seeds of its own improvement. Perfectionism always
> ends in a blind alley, while completeness by itself lacks selective
> values. (Jung, 1976a, p. 395)

Few of us realize that we do not see unmodified images of people,
especially of women, in magazines, film, or television. The images of
those we see as ideals, as possessing the looks we should aspire to, are

not real. We do not see those women as we would see them were we to encounter them in the supermarket or on the street. Images are manipulated to smooth out irregularities, alter color, define the waist, alter the dimensions of the body. When on rare occasions a model or actress shows unretouched photos, often the differences are glaringly obvious, enough that many of us would not recognize them on the street. We are bombarded with altered images—2,000–5,000 per week according to Susie Orbach (2009, p. 109) of images that "convey an idea of a body which does not exist in the real world." Cosmetic surgery as a means to attain this non-existent ideal flourishes in this environment. Since 1997, the number of cosmetic surgery procedures has grown from 1,679,943 procedures to 15.1 million procedures in 2013 (American Society of Plastic Surgeons, 2014a). What is the result? As Orbach says,

> Cosmetic surgery as a consumer option is becoming normalised. The young discuss the procedures they will have. A rhetoric of empowerment supports and provokes their desires and suggests that not to alter themselves would be a sign of self-neglect … The surgeon, both authoritative and solicitous, becomes the arbiter on female beauty. As he acknowledges the pain his patients feel, he demonstrates how he can change different aspects of their body for them, enabling them to reach the beauty standard he has himself set. In his engagement with them, he gives them the body they could never imagine they would have. He is confident and persuasive. He responds to their wish with gravity but also as though they were choosing their dream holiday. (Orbach, 2009, p. 103)

The beauty industry and the diet industry reap profits in the billions of dollars each year as women pursue the hopeless quest of achieving the perfection of the images placed in front of us thousands of time each week, of sleek flawless bodies which seem never to age. Young women and girls now diet and exercise stringently trying to achieve a thigh gap, a space between the thighs which somehow has become another aspect of beauty, one achievable by practically no one without losing enough weight to verge on anorexic. It is worth noting that ninety percent of cosmetic surgeons, the "arbiter[s] on female beauty," are male (PR leap, 2013) and ninety-one percent of patients seeking such surgery are female (American Society of Plastic Surgeons, 2014b). All of us fall short of perfection as we must. Is there no way for a person simply to be fat, without it being an indicator for some kind of pathology? Is there no way that I, a fat person, can be whole as I am? Indeed this is a fundamental issue. To assert wholeness and be fat is an act of courage.

I started out taking the stance of the fat acceptance and Health At Every Size (HAES) movements on this question, namely that Woodman and Orbach and the rest are all off the track in pathologising fat, seeing it as a pathological medical, psychological, and social phenomenon. Under the mantra of treatment and prevention, fatness is a problem that requires a solution, that is, the physical reduction of the fat body, and the elimination of the potential for individuals to become fat. And they (the fat activists) have a point, because fat is not in and of itself evidence of pathology, as is widely assumed. But when being fat intersects and occurs with the complexes Woodman explores, then fat symbolically becomes a visible manifestation of those complexes and the emotions they are associated with. For a fat person, for me, to be whole as I am, I have to come to terms with the body I have—embrace it, inhabit it, cherish it, live fully in it—and do the work of minimizing the negative effects of those complexes. The complexes are not unique to fat people, though being fat brings another dimension to them because of cultural stigma attached to it. This is a departure from Woodman, who sees fat as a symptom in the traditional sense, as indicative of something wrong. From the dictionary we know that a symptom is a physical or mental feature indicating the presence of disease. Looking at fat symbolically does not require an association with disease and takes us instead into the realm of meaning.

I write those words and I feel brave and full of hope that I can find freedom, wholeness in a combination of fat acceptance and working through my complexes. And I even have moments of patting myself on the back. Then I bump into it all again and I find myself feeling ugly, ashamed of my body, outside of life. All it takes is an instant of terrible self-consciousness and there I am. In my head I hear Leonard Cohen singing his song "Everybody knows. ..." Everybody knows fat women are ridiculous, ugly, undesirable. Everybody knows that. I search Google images for the word "fat people" on Google image. I look at them and my body tenses and tears come. I feel sad and enraged and sick all at the same time. It doesn't matter whether or not I am as fat or fatter than any of those people, because viscerally I know that under the domination of this fat complex we live in, I am one of them. That's what makes the Sam Keen piece that I discussed earlier piece so awful for me. He sees a woman who probably weighs around what I do and describes her, sees her, as "a parade of mammoth and grotesque proportions." Am I that? I feel horror at being viewed that way. How do I leave the house if that is how people see me? I remember moments when I felt pretty and I think I must have been delusional because everybody knows that is not possible. When I fall into this—fat complex—I feel I have to not have a body at all to sit across from my analyst because otherwise I will be swallowed up with the shame and rage and horror of what I fear he sees, how he sees me. When this happens, I don't want to see him again, for him to see me. Or I don't want to go out to a restaurant. Or any place where my body will be on view. Fortunately I am able to regain my ground again, but even as I do, I know there will be other moments of falling into the complex.

In this intersection of my negative mother complex and all the rest of those complexes and the fat bigotry that is around and in me every day, I have trouble finding my own solid ground. I can be angry about the things people like Keen write and say but that is a feeble defense because those words go right into my center. I can scream in outrage at those awful images on Google, but actually I have no shield against them. They go right into that vulnerable place inside, to the me who is and was my mother's little girl, the mistake.

I could go on and on quibbling about Bryant's "defect in the structure of the self." I can mount good intellectual arguments about the fallacy of placing anorexia and obesity on the same continuum. But that is all bravado. Can I be whole and fat? I believe I can. I must believe I can. I have to know it is possible. The stigma of being fat fits so perfectly into my complexes that I don't see where one stops and the other begins. That it takes so little to tip me over into this morass of self-loathing tells me I have more work to do. It seems a Fat Complex is at the heart of all of this. Perhaps Woodman should have explored that one.

As Woodman recognizes, "obesity and anorexia nervosa are counter- poles of one neurosis." For instance, in the home there is both a "clinging dependency" and "rigid control"; the daughter is not loved for herself and her own individuality. Emotions are repressed; the child is overly compliant and "too desirous to fulfill their parents' expectations", a "basic disturbance in self-awareness and body awareness," also the inability to recognize hunger as well as other bodily sensations. Typically the eating disturbance begins at puberty when the menstrual cycle commences. The girl attempts to gain control over her life through eating or through refusing to eat. Yet her ego is probably weak; there may be the danger of a psychotic break. Food seems to serve as a defense against depression, however, and the suicide rate is significantly lower for the obese. There is an impressive difference in how the obese and anorexic girls feel about themselves since the anorexic feels accepted by the culture as she is thin whereas the obese girl feels unaccepted and unacceptable by the culture. Although the anorexic becomes rebellious and stubborn in her teens the obese girl tends to remain outwardly compliant. The obese girl feels the terror of deprivation as much or more than the terror of being fat ... The obese girl feels a constant failure as she is unable to lose weight and suffers continual rejection from others. (Bryant, 1981, p. 35)

I feel almost unable to respond to this summation of Woodman by Bryant. It feels to me too sweeping in its assumptions. Take this—"there may be the danger of a psychotic break"—Am I to imagine from this that there are girls and women who literally become psychotic unless they are fat, that losing weight brings on psychosis? Where does this come from and what evidence is there? As with her assertion that there is a defect in the structure of the self, she is using words that arouse alarm but she offers no support for what she says.

This is *my* body. I look like my father's sisters and mother—round bodies, not one of them thin. This is MY body. My body expresses my neurosis? I am resisting again, wanting to quibble with what makes me uncomfortable, wanting to break the links, like a child clamping her mouth shut against some foul tasting medicine. I struggle to take in that my weight has symbolic meaning and value in my life, that it relates to my struggles with my mother, but still, this *is* my body. How do I take those things in without also feeling that I have made myself this way? I feel a judgment that underlies all of what I read of Woodman. It never comes out into the open, but the judgment is that I cannot be fat and not be neurotic. Something tells me that the way fat and neurosis travel together is not as Woodman sees it, though they do indeed often travel together. How could I find and accept that I have made myself this way and not also hate myself? I cannot and I feel like I am trying to walk a tightrope made of barbed wire when I try.

If not judgment, then maybe what I detect in Woodman is what feels like a kind of magical thinking, that doing the work of untangling the complexes will result in a change in the body, namely the fat will go away. I understand that wish. I lived with it and tortured myself with it for a long time. But that makes the fat body one big symptom. She may not herself be saying that doing the work will lead to becoming slender, but I feel fairly confident that belief is in there.

The standard recommendation for fat people is to diet. The assumption is that dieting will lead to weight loss and once lost, provided the fat person is vigilant, the loss will be maintained. Decades of dieting failed to make me thin. As it turns out, that is not my fault and I am not alone in my failure as it appears that diets simply do not work (Ferdman, 2015). Medicare paid for a study to determine what method of weight loss was best. The conclusion?

> You can initially lose 5 to 10 percent of your weight on any number of diets, but then the weight comes back. We found that the majority of people regained all the weight, plus more. Sustained weight loss was found only in a small minority of participants, while complete weight regain was found in the majority. Diets do not lead to sustained weight loss or health benefits for the majority of people ... In addition, the studies do not provide consistent evidence that dieting results in significant health improvements, regardless of weight change. In sum, there is little support for the notion that diets lead to lasting weight loss or health benefits. (Mann et al., 2007, p. 233)

It is not a matter of finding the right diet—they all fail and it is not my fault.

I can't become thin without endangering my life. I could apply for weight loss surgery and they would accept me. It wouldn't matter that I would be risking my life to be thin. That I would be voluntarily mutilating my body, making myself subject to all kinds of side effects and nutritional deficiencies so that other people could look at me and feel okay. How is that sane, especially when you consider that even with surgery, the weight often comes back? I am healthy now. I have every reason to expect I will live at least into my mid eighties, but if I were willing to risk my life and have that damned surgery and I lost fifteen to twenty-five percent of my body weight, which is the average lost after surgery, then I would be seen as healthy and good and not neurotic? That makes no sense to me.

Bariatric surgery is sold as a "whole new me," a radical makeover. This before-and-after sales pitch is part of the surgery's appeal to fat people who are desperately trying to manage weight stigma. But when you listen to people who are beyond the one-year "honeymoon" stage, the truth about what surgery changes and what it doesn't is more apparent. At that point we see that the suicide rate is six to seven times higher for people who have had the surgery than those who did not (Alexander, 2008). Bariatric surgery does not make you a new person. It does not permanently get rid of sleep apnea, diabetes, etc., which are completely treatable without the surgery. It does not even usually turn fat people into thin people—the average weight loss leaves most patients still in the "obese" range, and weight regain is the norm, though it is slower than weight regain after dieting. It requires adhering forever to a restrictive diet and taking multiple supplements to deal with the nutritional deficiencies that result from interfering with the normal digestive process. And this is preferable to being fat?

I can only imagine how terrible it must be to undergo surgery with all the hopes of finally becoming "like everyone else," enduring the difficulties of adjusting to the requirements of post-surgery eating, only to lose far less than expected and start to regain the weight lost at such great cost. That the suicide risk is increased hardly seems surprising.

I wish I were amazed that while female circumcision is condemned for interfering with sexual pleasure and mutilating women's bodies and causing a lifetime of complications, bariatric surgery is seen as positive, a move toward health despite the fact that it interferes with pleasure, mutilates women's—and men's—bodies and causes a lifetime of complications. In an increasingly popular form of bariatric surgery, the gastric sleeve procedure most of the stomach is removed, amputated leaving only a tube behind. This procedure is not reversible. A *healthy* organ is mutilated in this procedure.

Or consider this: the inventor of the Segway applied for approval for a device he calls AspireAssist which is medical device with a tube which is surgically implanted in the stomach and is attached to a skin-port which is equipped with a valve which is attached to a battery operated pump which sucks a portion of your stomach contents out of your gut and mechanically vomits them into your toilet. (The aspire assist, n.d.) In a thin or normal weight person, induced vomiting after eating is considered an eating disorder, purging which is a part of anorexia and bulimia, and seen as a health hazard and psychiatric disorder. In a fat person, a device that does this is seen as treatment. I actually thought that the FDA would recognize this device for what it is, but I was wrong. Last week, with much ballyhoo, AspireAssist actually received FDA approval. The *New York Times* headline—"FDA approves stomach-draining obesity treatment" (Chicago Tribune, 2016)—makes me want to shout ARE YOU KIDDING? Can only we fish who see the water see the madness in this?

Given the decidedly mixed outcome from bariatric surgery—the increased risk of suicide, serious post-operative complications, and only modest weight loss—how can it be seriously argued that this is all about concern for my health? Is it not more about making me aesthetically more appealing to others? Is it not about showing dramatically that I agree that my body is as offensive as others believe? And if these procedures are curative of Type 2 diabetes, then why are they not recommended for all Type 2 diabetes patients? If medical rather than surgical treatment is the preferred option for non-obese Type 2 diabetes patients, why should it not also be for all such patients? Samantha Murray connects the dots:

> As I noted earlier, with the help of Helen Keane, eating is experienced as a compulsive activity precisely because of the expectation of restraint from those who are instructed they are fat. Given this, a surgery that offers relief from the effort and scrutiny involved in dieting via the insertion of a device that institutes control forcibly, and at an unconscious, physiological level, seems a viable solution. (Murray, 2009)

It feels to me that my "neurosis," at least as related to being fat per se, stems from trying to adapt, trying to compensate for having this fat body, trying to defeat this body that will not be thin. Woodman says, "Fat in our culture is taboo … The fat girl is not one with her peers … In short, in our society she is not a female and no one knows it as well as she" (Bryant, 1981, p. 30). Under those conditions, about which she is correct, how could a person not become neurotic? In the world of chickens and eggs, Woodman would have it that my fat body is the neurosis and it feels to me like the neurosis comes from having this body. I mean here that Woodman says my body is the indicator of my neurosis, is how it plays out and I am trying to say that having a fat body creates neurosis, because of being different, because of all the social condemnation and judgment, all of the futile efforts to make it smaller. The two most obvious choices for a fat woman are either: (1) lie on the Procrustean bed and literally, through bariatric surgery, have herself cut down to size, or figuratively try to do so through constant dieting and food deprivation, or (2) become defiant and embrace being fat, revel in being fat with the same verve that she previously hated her fat and her body. Both smell of neurosis to me.

> Thinness, exploited by advertising, [has become] a bogeyman, a judge, an accuser, an impossible standard, a drain on women's emancipatory goals. The advertised image of thinness, closely associated with beauty and "health" has become central to the notion of a "good woman" who is "trying her best" to look right, live right and be right. Although … advertised thinness on the surface promises that woman can "have it all" … its most powerful, secret message is to remind them of their subordinate status as women, still judged on the basis of their bodies. They must take up less space, fit into prescribed molds of standardized beauty, restrain their desires by discipline their hungry bodies. No one wants a fat woman, someone out of "control". (Gutwill, 1994a, p. 12)

There is a difference between the fat body and the obese body. The term obese places the fat body in the realm of pathological. Obesity does not meet the definition of disease, despite the recent action of the AMA. It is also not a diagnostic category in the DSM V, though now that the AMA, overriding its own scientific panel, has declared obesity a disease, I expect that soon it will be so classified in the next version.

> Obesity, defined as a body mass index (BMI, kg/m^2) or percentage body fat in excess of some cut-off value, though clearly a threat to health and longevity, lacks a universal concomitant group of symptoms or signs and the impairment of function which characterize disease according to traditional definitions. While it might nevertheless be possible to achieve a social consensus that it is a disease despite its failure to fit traditional models of disease, the merits of such a goal are questionable. Labeling obesity a disease may be

expedient but it is not a necessary step in a campaign to combat obesity and it may be interpreted as self-serving advocacy without a sound scientific basis. (Heska, 2001, p. 1401)

Woodman is right when she says that fat is taboo. Being fat means living every day with knowing that in the eyes of many, I am not a legitimate woman, not acceptable. Most clothing stores don't want my business and say that by not carrying clothing in my size. It is extremely difficult to maintain a secure sense of self, to walk about with pride and comfort, secure in being a woman, under such circumstances.

> **Woodman:** ... *In short, in our society she is not a female and no one knows it as well as she. Isolation forces her into her own inner world where fantasies compensate for the unlived life and the images of the imagination gradually take on a numinous power.* (Woodman, 1982, p. 22)

Marion, I get this. For a long time I refrained from doing things that would expose me to the painful reality she describes. The girl who didn't date in high school, who was the friend and not the girlfriend, the girl who didn't dance. But nearly all of the writers I have cited say this very same thing, that to be fat is to be illegitimate, a failed citizen.

> **Woodman:** *For Jung ... To become conscious of the body was to become conscious of the spirit ... Bearing this in mind, obesity must be understood in terms of the symbol. In that understanding lies the treatment and the possibility for healing.* (Woodman, 1980, p. 60)

But what is healing? What does fat symbolize? I don't have a single point from which to see it. Inside myself, when I quiet the critical attacking voice, my large body symbolizes power, abundance, life, fecundity. It is soft, cushiony, sensual, but from the outside or from those attacking voices, fat is too much, gluttony, greed, weakness, laziness, ugly. Is my body, just as it is, the way it is meant to be, as is my height and my eye color? For me, healing is to end the war within. To be able to be at home with myself in myself. To inhabit my body without shame.

CHAPTER EIGHT

Memory, shame, and the fat body—pulling it all together

Previously I wrote that I believe with all my Jungian heart that my fat is meaningful. It tells me that we develop symptoms when we are stuck in old patterns and fail to integrate creative potentials within our personality. Symptoms are not to be avoided or downplayed, but the meaning, which has often heretofore been missed, needs to be discovered in order for healing to take place. But that requires that my fat be a symptom of something, not a more basic state of being. The question remains—must it be a symptom in order to be meaningful, to have symbolic meaning for me?

Callan provocatively says:

> A symptom is an untended memory. It is the voice of a forgotten or banished part of ourselves ... Memory is the medicine of the psyche—even, and especially when the memories are dark. (Callan, 2004, p. 7)

I try this on. My fat is an untended memory. It is the voice of my negative relationship with my mother. Of my rage. My fears of dependency. Of abandonment. At least in part it is. Memory in the body. I recall master knitter Elizabeth Zimmerman said "One likes to believe that there is memory in the fingers; memory undeveloped, but still alive" (Zimmerman, 1981, p. 75). It is here that my delight in knitting, my foundation in analytical psychology and this work begin to meet in memory and the body. As Marie Louise Von Franz put it:

> Everybody who has knitted or done weaving or embroidery knows what an agreeable effect this can have, for you can be quiet and lazy and also spin your own thoughts while working. You can relax and follow your fantasy and then get up and say you have done something! (Von Franz, 1972, p. 40)

It is a given in current trauma theory that memory lives in the body and that the body carries the impact of trauma. Donald Kalsched writes:

> It is different with the victim of early trauma. For these patients, disowned material is not psychically represented, but has been banished to the body or relegated to discrete psychical fragments, between which amnesia barriers have been erected. It must never be allowed to return to consciousness. (Kalsched, 1997, p. 104)

Though it has been a struggle, through analysis I can see myself as one of the people Kalsched and psychoanalytic theorists like Phillip Bromberg write about. I used to think that I had a good memory for my childhood. In analysis, as I struggled to answer questions about what I remembered, I began to see that pieces were missing. I know my mother was often ill in my first four years and we were separated a lot—because she was in the hospital or I was away living with my grandmother or godmother. But I don't know when she was gone or for how long. I know that my father, due to his career in the Army, was gone a great deal of the time when I was four and the whole year that I was five and at times throughout my childhood. But I don't remember him leaving and I don't remember him returning. I have no memories of his actual departures or returns and there were many throughout my childhood. My memory consists of snapshots, quick flashes with gaps between shots, and I don't know how long the gaps were or what happened in them. I learned to live in my mind. I saw myself as peering out through my eyes, as if my body housed a very tiny being who lived entirely within my head.

A few years ago I dreamed:

> I am in my analyst's office talking with him. I am knitting as I talk. I'm making a large deep purple shawl, something to wrap myself in to keep me warm. I see a hole, a place where I made a mistake and I know I will have to take out several inches of work to get to it and fix the error, that a short cut won't work. He says this work is like that.

I am a knitter. Knitters come in two basic types. The project knitter buys yarn and pattern for a specific project and knits that and only that until it is finished. Process knitters knit to knit. We love to look at, touch and acquire yarn and usually have several projects going at the same time. The finished project is nice but it is the process, the knitting itself that is engaging. Sometimes the project is never completed or it is unraveled and the yarn used again for something else. I love the feel of the yarn as it slides through my fingers as I knit. I stop frequently and pull the fabric into shape and touch it and look at it and enjoy the color and shape. Knitting a sock, knit from top to toe with a single thread that is never broken, I marvel at the genius of the first person who figured out how to "turn the heel" and change the sock from a simple tube into something that hugs the form and shape of the human foot. These days I knit a lot of lace, knit with fine thread on small needles with intentional holes, for lace without holes is not lace at all.

In the dream, I am working with beautiful deep purple yarn. The yarn is deep rich purple, my favorite color. Purple the color of the vestments of Lent, a color of mourning. Purple, "the red of passion balanced by the blue of reason, or the real by the ideal, or love by wisdom, or earth by heaven, or, psychologically, the union of opposing energies within an individual" (ARAS, 2010, p. 694). The color of royalty. The color of an ancient dye made by the Phoenicians from the sea snail. The color of grapes, lavender, wisteria, iris, and violets. Purple is the color of the Crown chakra. "… the highest and most sacred values are represented by purple" (ARAS, 2010, p. 694).

I had a large quantity of this very yarn for some time, a soft and elegant yarn 100 percent cashmere, almost unimaginably soft to the touch. Lustrous and rich in feel and color. I had the yarn but couldn't find the right pattern, couldn't find what it wanted to be. I would look at it on the shelf with my cones of beautiful yarns and try to feel, to imagine what it should become. Then I had the dream, a dream about the purple yarn, analysis and my efforts to create something I can wrap myself in, something warm and soft. In the dream, I pause in my knitting to look at the fabric and see, several inches below where I am working, a hole, not a hole belonging to the pattern but a large hole, a hole that distorts the lace.

I am not a perfectionist with my knitting. When I find an error, I don't often rip out work done. I try to find some relatively easy way to fix it, to cover the error so no one will notice. But this hole in the shawl I am making from this yarn is one I cannot ignore or overlook. The knitter's adage that if a man galloping by on horseback can't spot a mistake, then it needn't be repaired just doesn't apply for this hole. In the dream, I know I will have to rip out several inches of knitting. Many lace knitters use safety lines, a contrasting yarn threaded through the stitches every few inches making ripping back easier. They rip back to the safety line and needn't fear losing stitches because they will be held by the line. I work without such a line. When I rip back, I must move slowly, stitch by stitch, paying as much, even more attention to the unknitting as I do to the knitting. Slow and painstaking work.

Some time after the dream, a designer who creates wonderfully intricate patterns that usually feature a lot of beads, announced a new design, one she called "In Dreams." And it was to be done in a mystery knit-along, with sections of the pattern made available every two weeks over a span of three months. As soon as I learned of it, I knew this was the project for this yarn. I had no picture to tell me what the final shawl would look like, only that it would be a semi-circle and have many beads. I had to be willing to knit each part as it became available and trust that the finished design would be pleasing to me and would suit my purposes.

I began. I completed the first section. But the beads were wrong, too large and not the color I wanted. So, I ripped it out and began again. This time a significant error appeared right near the beginning. Ripped it out again. Finally, I completed the first clue and began the second. The work went along without incident until near the end of the clue, when I discovered an error. I had to slowly and tediously take out several rows, nearly an inch of work. I had to pay careful attention as I came to each beaded stitch lest I lose the beads, and there were nearly 100 of them, tiny beads, in each row in this section. I fixed the error and then discovered I had made it again, in the same place. Three times I had to unknit that inch of work. Three times I had to work not to lose a bead or drop a stitch. Finally, on the fourth attempt I succeeded in completing the pattern section. There were five more sections yet to come. And then another large error. I had to rip it out again. This was not smooth going.

I used to knit sweaters, for me, for my children, for my husband, and afghans (blankets). Then for a long time I mostly knitted socks. These days I am drawn only to knitting lace, the more intricate the design, the larger the stole or shawl, the better. What does it mean that I want only to knit designs with deliberate holes in them? Donald Kalsched tells us, "Memory has holes. A full narrative history cannot be told by an individual whose life has been disrupted by trauma" (Kalsched, 1996, p. 13). In my dream I am knitting a lace shawl as I do in waking life after the dream. In the midst of the intentional holes that shape the pattern of the lace appears a misplaced hole, a mistaken hole. Memory has holes, holes that both shape the pattern and disrupt it, as in my dream.

The word "memory" comes to us from the middle English/Anglo-French word *memorie*, and from the Latin *memoria*, derived from *memor*, which means "mindful." It comes from an Indo-European root *smer*—which in one form refers to grease and fat. How is memory connected to "fat"? Think about how difficult it is to get rid of fat. Russell Lockhart writes, "It sticks. It adheres. It won't leave. It leaves traces. A memory is what sticks, what adheres in the mind. Memory is the fat of the mind" (Lockhart, 2012, p. 188). Related words that share the history of memory include remember, commemorate, memorable, memento, and memorandum. The word mourn also shares its derivations. The same root that gave rise to memory gives rise to mourn. Lockhart continues:

> When someone has passed away or slipped away, we mourn. When we are in mourning, we are deeply engaged with the memory of that person. Our mind is full of memories. We can only mourn through memory and with memory. We mourn for what we had and can now have only in memory. (Lockhart, 2012, p. 189)

Memory, mourning, and fat.

I pick up what I have been knitting and it contains memory. I see what the day was when last I knit on this piece. My hairs get knitted into the fabric as do my cats' hairs. The daydreams dreamed, the worries worried, the interior dialogues are all there, part of the fabric that I knit.

Each piece carries my life knit into it, its fabric also the fabric of my memory. I am knitting lace. I am doing analysis. There I am working on knitting the lace of my life, repairing holes that don't belong, trying to work out the pattern.

Estes writes:

> The body remembers, the bones remember, the joints remember, even the little finger remembers. Memory is lodged in pictures and feelings in the cells themselves. Like a sponge filled with water, anywhere the flesh is pressed, wrung, even touched lightly, a memory may flow out in a stream. (Estes, 1992, p. 200)

The wrestling with Woodman is all about memory and connecting, linking with grief, rage, need, and desire. My resistance to her, to the links she makes between fat and those complexes is my resistance to those feelings long buried in my fat itself. Estes argues:

> Though we hate to admit it, over and over again, the poorest bargain of our lives is the one we make when we forfeit our deep knowing life for one that is far more frail; when we give up our teeth, our claws, our sense, our scent; when we surrender our wilder natures for a promise of something that seems rich but turns out to be hollow ... we make this bargain without realizing the sorrow, the pain, and the dislocation it will cause us. (Estes, 1992, p. 394)

So is my fat a symptom of my negative mother complex? Of my rage? Of my deep dependency needs? Of my fear of abandonment? All of the above? Even as resistant as I am, it must be, at least in part, all of these things. Maybe. Or maybe it's all of those things and something more. Maybe my fat is itself a trauma, maybe it is being fat, the lived experience day in and day out of inhabiting my fat body that is the trauma, rather than fat being symptomatic of trauma.

If I do not give in to my resistance, then I could say that my fat is made up of all my swallowed fury and that if I let it all out, I would shrink, deflate like a punctured balloon.

That I am fat because underneath I feel like I have no substance at all, nothing but mind because I don't have that body-memory of being held and seen and known and loved. I have no body memory, just pictures in my mind. Inside me there is no one, no body, just thoughts, just mind. I feel like I have no body inside my fat. I cover up my absence, my lack, bury my bodily feelings and memories with mass.

I wanted to be seen—that is why I am fat, so I am seen.

I dream about a famine. The famine I am actually in is about love, want, and need. I am fat so no one would suspect I am starving, but I am. I go into my mind to satisfy my hunger but thoughts can't do it.

An image comes to me. I imagine a slender woman stepping in and out of a fat body. My body is dumb, slow, heavy, weighed down by its mass. Unloved, seldom touched, carrying memories forgotten and feelings not felt. Mass surrounding and protecting the inner and very vulnerable core. The slender woman, my mind, is quick, silver, bright. Mercurial, lithe, electric. The fat woman has a great hollow space at her center; the silver woman has no substance. They resent each other. Each believes she is the real me. In my body, I feel heavy, dumb, slow, ugly. I want to be hugged and when I imagine it, I see myself as a troll, an ugly, misshapen mass that can only disgust. Yet in my mind I am grace-ful and even pretty, sparkling, bright, appealing, silvery. So long as I stay alone, so long as my contact with others is virtual—by telephone or online, I can be my mind and escape the lump of flesh that is my body.

I had a dream about being interviewed by a small group of people, as I was fifteen years ago by a committee at the Jung Institute. The inter-viewer asks me about my weight. I tell her a good part of the problem is what they assume they know about me because I am fat.

Now I could say more. That my weight tells the story about my rela-tionship with my mother. About my need. About my fear of abandon-ment. About my rage at a husband who would not love me. At a father who left me and didn't protect me and then denied me. My rage at myself. That I have had to wear all of this because I could not digest it. My weight also tells of the long line of women from whom I am descended that I look just like. Of my genetic endowment. And it is who I am.

Or now I would ask if they want me to defend my body and why should anyone have to defend the body that they are?

Or I would respond with telling them what it is like to live in a world that reviles fat and my body, that tells me every day that I am ugly, lazy, undisciplined, out of control, gluttonous and slothful. And ask why they don't ask about that, about what it is like to be part of a stigmatized group? Why they don't ask me how I see that history shaping me, much as they might ask a gay person something similar?

I like to think I would respond very differently now.

Another voice in me chimes in. It all seems so unfair. Surely other women have had such difficult mothers, missing-in-action fathers, and unhappy marriages and do not become fat, if those things are where my fat comes from. And surely there are fat people with wonderful mothers, supportive fathers and solid loving marriages. My mind whirls with trying to make sense of it all. But I know that they don't matter, because I had a negative mother and an often-absent father and an unhappy marriage, all of which are part of my fat, right there with my genetic heritage.

The figure so often trumpeted about how much obesity costs in health care, a figure in the billions of dollars per year, seems to be derived by assuming that the cause of all health expenditures for any fat person is fat. Which is like saying dark skin is the real cause of such expenditures for all African Americans. Dr. Mehmet Oz says all of his fat patients have heart disease. We are supposed to nod in agreement with this sage observation of his. But wait—of course all of his fat patients have heart disease because *he is a heart surgeon and cardiologist*. Why would anyone, fat or thin be seeing him if they did not have heart disease? Now it feels like any and every complex and emotional issue is the reason for my fat. Any therapist or analyst could say that all of their fat patients have mother complexes. Like Mehmet Oz, they would be guilty of confirmation bias. Imagine a slender woman with a strongly negative mother—I see them in my practice so I know they exist. I don't assume, and no one does, that she is slender because of her mother. But I am to accept that my fat is the physical substance of my mother complex, father complex, food complex, and my bad marriage? Why is that true only for fat people? I follow Woodman's arguments and I see myself in them, but what, it seems to me, that I see are the complexes, not how they are my fat. My resistance bubbles up again and I want to ask why, what is the mechanism that made my anger become fat? I don't understand. And no one can answer me. If my fat symbolizes those complexes, how are those complexes symbolized in slender people? Is that my resistance talking? I want to defend myself against this painful knowing that for me, my fat is a physical manifestation of all of these things in my life. Had I not had the parents I had, the unhappy marriage I had, the fears and anxieties I suffered, I would not be the me, the Cheryl I know and am now. I likely would not be slender, but my body would not be carrying the same weight of my experience. Along with those things, an essential piece of who I am, of this Cheryl, is my fat and all that it has been and continues to be for me. I am not some generic fat person. I am me, Cheryl, who is fat, bright, had a difficult childhood, an unhappy marriage, and always an ambivalent relationship with my body.

How do I not feel crushed by the weight of blame for my own body? That is where this work brings me. To this place of knowing, in a place deep inside myself, that I am in part the architect of my body. The struggle now is to accept that without blame, without the judgment and shame that blame brings with it. Some days it's easier than others.

Woodman brings me back to this intersection of memory and my body:

> ... the fat body may be both a womb and a tomb. If she sees it as a tomb, the woman may be too ready to give up her search for her own life force which is buried alive within her. If she has the courage to look in the mirror and actually see her own dark side—without identifying with it—she may be able to see her fatness symbolically, and thus find the objectivity to suffer the pain of awareness. (Woodman, 1980, p. 42)

The hardest part of this, harder than accepting that I am not an innocent victim of my biology, is facing my unlived life. The career I abandoned— yes, I became a psychotherapist as I wanted to, but the other part of my professional identity, the part where I was seen as a student with promise, one who could perhaps have made a mark or found her way to analytic training, that part didn't happen. Because I killed it when I chose to marry the first time and abandon my own ambition and enterprise in order to try to persuade him to love me and build the future I imagined. In fact, that imagined life became more powerful as the real one was not working. I made myself believe that we were good parents together, good friends, and colleagues and that somehow it didn't matter so much that we were only married in the legal sense.

I look at photos of myself in the year I got married and I don't understand how I could have seen myself as undesirable. I see a pretty young woman with dark hair and big brown eyes. She is the woman my husband said he would love when she got down to 120 pounds. She is the woman he, and I, saw as fat. It's as if I looked into a funhouse mirror that reflected back a distorted image that I accepted as real. I saw myself reflected in the eyes of the man I married and men who weren't attracted to me and their view became my distorted image of myself, as fat, unattractive, and unwantable.

So I didn't date, didn't dance, didn't flirt. I stayed on the sidelines watching with envy as my friends did what I wanted to and believed I could not. Which led me to marry a man who could not, would not tell me he loved me. A man I married because I was afraid that as a fat girl, he was the best I could get, that I had to settle for someone who was willing to have children with me, even if he did not really love me. What I did not realize the very first night we slept together was that he was not only saying that sleeping with me didn't mean he loved me, but that it also meant that marrying and having children with me did not make me his heart's desire either.

And more. Before I applied for analytic training, two analysts—one, my first analyst, the other, someone I did supervision with for three years—told me that though they thought I would make a good analyst, they said I would be turned down for training because of my weight. I went into those interviews carrying their prediction. After all they had both been involved with the training committee so they must know what they were talking about, or so I believed. Then when I was rejected, I gave up on being an analyst. My weight might well be part of why I was rejected, though likely not the only reason, but it was what I felt. I didn't know how to bounce back from that rejection. The same thing that made me believe that I was unwantable made me believe I couldn't find an opening any place else. I took the rejection from the Jung Institute as a statement about my value and assumed that any institute would see me the same way. I opted instead for an easy way out by going back to school and completing my doctorate. A degree that was a distant second choice for me.

I have to swallow all of that. I did my doctoral work on Medea. It was the Medea in me who killed the children that were my ambitions.

Mother, father, anger, food. It is a banquet of bitter foods I must eat in this process.

What does this mean for me? My body is the result of genes, environment, history, experience. And yes, my complexes. Had I different genetic endowment, those complexes likely would find expression in some other way, through alcohol or drug abuse, perhaps. Or high-risk behaviors.

I come to the end of my effort to apply Woodman's ideas to my own history. I admit to feeling some ambivalence about it. On the one hand,

I see the complexes she emphasizes present in me. There is no denying that. But Woodman presumes to be speaking about all fat women and within this assumes all fat women are compulsive eaters, all fat women are hiding in their fat, assumes all fat women can be thin and if they don't want to be or they fail to become thin, it is a psychological issue. She believes that fatness is the other side of the coin to anorexia. I know what she says is not true of all fat women. And I know that some of it is true of me. Woodman sees cause where I see co-occurrence. Having a negative mother complex, father complex, and the rest are neither necessary nor sufficient to cause a person to be fat. But when they occur together with fat, they do indeed amplify pain and suffering. I know this from my own life.

Must I see my fat body as unnatural, as a shape that is not mine?

A friend asked where I am with all of this, how I feel now. I feel sad, mostly about life I did not live because of my fears. I see my own history more clearly and feel it more deeply.

I feel angry at all the prejudice that surrounds me, so angry that sometimes I want to shout at people who repeat the usual nostrums that allegedly will make a fat person thin. Someone once said that the anger of all the fat women is enough to burn the world. I feel that anger.

I've looked at where my fat comes from and wrestled with what it means—I continue to wrestle with it. Where am I with all of this? I am a fat woman in a world that reviles fat. Which means that I am under constant scrutiny yet rarely visible as a person, as a woman. I never fit in as I might were I slender. My experience being in my body is different from that of a woman who feels the admiring glance of men as she moves through the world, who needs never check the width of chairs before sitting, who can go into any clothing store for women and find things that fit her, who doesn't have to prepare her defense of her body any time she sees a new doctor. We both likely feel less at home in our bodies than either of us would like and can reel off features we wish were different, and we both face all the problems that any woman dealing with a world that still privileges men faces. This isn't to say that anyone should feel sorry for me, only that being fat means dealing with an additional set of biases and problems than a slender person confronts. Some days I feel that more than others.

As I write this, it is late spring. In warm weather I like to wear full skirts and dresses. As I look at summer dresses in the catalogs and websites of the places that carry clothes in my size, I see with dismay that most of the dresses I like are sleeveless. For all the work I have done to come to terms with and embrace my body, for all that I have embraced fat acceptance and eschewed dieting and body loathing, there remains a pocket of shame about my body that gets reawakened every summer—I have very fat upper arms and though there is no sleeve that would hide that fact or make my arms look slender, the thought of baring them in a sleeveless dress fills me with anxiety and shame. It is as if every bit of shame and anxiety about revealing my body becomes located in my arms and only if I keep them covered, can I dare go out into the world. I seize upon this wonderful quote: "when it comes to dressing myself, i live by a very simple principle. i am fat, therefore, i look fat in everything; consequently, i can wear anything." (Selling, 2013). I chuckle and I get it but still, sleeveless? How could I move about in the world knowing there is no way for my invisibility cloak to hide my arms? All this work and the thought of showing my arms undoes me. The work goes on. I support the right to bare arms. Maybe next summer my arms can go bare.

Marion Woodman would have fat people do the work of becoming conscious of the various complexes she sees implicated in fat. But she could not see her own participation in the cultural fat complex. Samuel Kimbles says about resolving this complex:

> If we do not sort through our cultural as well as personal complexes carefully, we end up—at a minimum in the unconscious—feeling responsible for, identified with, or traumatized by events that belong to our cultural complexes far more than our personal complexes. Failure to consider cultural complexes as part of the work of individuation puts a tremendous burden on both the personal and archetypal realms of the psyche. Placing such a burden on the personal and/or archetypal dimensions by ignoring the careful sorting out of cultural complexes does not allow for the freeing up of the tremendous energy held in the grip of cultural complexes and making it available for the development of healthier individuals and groups, who are able to have positive interaction with other groups and cultures. Too often the Jungian notion/bias of "differentiating out from the collective" in the service of individuation does not take into account either the role of cultural complexes in development or the need to make a place for oneself in the life of the group or a place for one's group in relation to other groups. (Singer, 2004, p. 33)

Woodman is certainly not alone in wanting fat people to do the work of changing. In the March 2014 issue of the *Journal of Health Psychology* Seacat (Seacat, Dougal, & Roy, 2014) reports the results of his team's study on the incidence of fat shaming, a study done by asking fifty fat women to keep a daily diary of weight stigmatizing events. Not unexpectedly the results show that such stigmatizing incidents are common—1,077 of them in a week reported by his subjects. Like Woodman and so many others, Seacat believes it falls to fat people to develop the skills and the courage to face those daily barriers they encounter and keep going, for fat people to do the work rather than calling for directing serious effort to change these attitudes if only among the helping professions.

CHAPTER NINE

My body, my self:
toward a theory of fat and trauma

Almost every approach to working with the fat patient in psychotherapy involves the notion that her fat is the result of trauma in the past and that the answer lies in losing weight, becoming less fat or even better stop being fat at all. But what happens if we begin to think instead that her fat, rather than being a response to trauma or any of the several complexes Woodman outlines, what if her fat is itself a source of trauma, of being fat? What if we look at the effect on the psyche of being visibly different, visibly part of an "injured group"?

We know that for African Americans, their visible difference from the normative dominant white culture creates a host of anxieties and behaviors. In the days following the Trayvon Martin verdict, I watched and listened as prominent African Americans spoke of their fears for their own children, knowing that privileged status was no protection against racial hostility and fear. On a visceral level I understood their anxiety, their knowing that always, no matter what, they must remain aware that they are different, they are outside the white mainstream, just as I, no matter my accomplishments, am always seen as fat and thus I am also always on guard against the bias that I encounter every day because I am fat. As is true for African Americans, I cannot escape my difference, my outsider status, because I wear it, my status is visible all the time.

Samantha Murray writes of her reaction to an account of a particularly abhorrent sexual practice among young male military cadets involving a fat woman. She recalls her reaction as she listened to the paper in which the account was reported:

> I suddenly became acutely aware of my own fat bulges and folds. I imagined every eye in the room on me, shaking their heads in pity, revulsion and even morbid curiosity. I pulled my shirt surreptitiously away from the bulges of my belly and my hips, trying to separate the appearance from the reality. I shifted in my chair, and felt my cheeks burn hot and my stomach churn. I was angry, so angry, so humiliated for the fat girl who had suffered at the hands of these young boys: she was just a girl, a girl like I was and had been, and she had been made into a ravenous, libidinous, ridiculous creature. And yet I was ashamed. I was aware of the disgust my body inspired, its complete unacceptability and invisibility in the sexual domain, apart from as a figure of ridicule. I felt hot tears sting my eyes, and I knew I had to get out. I squeezed my wide hips between the rows of chairs, and fled the room.
>
> It was not that I did not realise that society does not think fatness is sexy. It was not that I had never had the experience of being relegated to the category of the asexual "big girl" or been laughed at, or positioned as sexually undesirable. It was that this story was so illustrative of these attitudes and so callous and violent in the way they were played out. I could reason things out along lines that fatness was not abhorrent to everyone, that this kind of cruelty was the exception rather than the rule ... But in the midst of this reason, *I experienced myself as split.* ... I felt carved up, split in two: I felt that any conception of myself as a sexual being was ridiculous, and could only be imagined in my mind, never acted out by my body. I felt radically disconnected from my own flesh, my own sexuality. (Murray, 2004, pp. 237–239) [Emphasis mine]

There it was, a description of splitting, of the dissociative defense so much a part of the lives of people with trauma histories. I saw a link to the effects of trauma as explored by Donald Winnicott, Donald Kalsched, Bessel van der Kolk, and Philip Bromberg.

It has been assumed by some writing about obesity that one of the causes is a trauma history, that becoming fat is a defense against a reaction to trauma. Indeed this is essentially what Woodman asserts and it may well be true. But Murray, in her description of her experience of splitting from her body, opened for me another possibility—that it is being fat, being on the receiving end of the bias, stigmatization, vilification that comes of being fat that is a current trauma, a trauma which remains present every day so long as one is fat. The fat woman who has a trauma history of abuse or neglect, for example, has not only the effects of the trauma of the past as they bubble up and influence her life in the present to deal with but also the trauma of being deviant, of having a stigmatized body and she faces this trauma every day, every time she steps outside her home. Neither trauma can be erased as history cannot be rewritten and bodies resist reshaping so the task is to learn to recognize the effects of the trauma and develop means to cope and live fully.

Bessel van der Kolk describes the process of splitting in abused children:

> As a result, abused children are likely to grow up believing that they are fundamentally unlovable; that was the only way their young minds could explain why they were treated so badly. They survive by denying, ignoring, and splitting off large chunks of reality: They forget the abuse; they suppress their rage or despair; they numb their physical sensations. (van der Kolk, 2015, p. 281)

Though he is describing the process in children it is easily observable in fat people, as Murray relates or as any fat woman can tell you what she must do to be able to walk down the street. Day in and day out, fat people are bombarded with messages that they are unwantable and often unlovable, even. My "invisibility cloak" has been my way of "denying, ignoring and splitting off" chunks of the reality that I as a fat woman encounter when I leave the comfort of my home, my fat space.

Philip Bromberg, in *Awakening the Dreamer*, offers this look at the process of dealing with trauma:

> With trauma, we must remember, retelling means reliving. Yet it is only through its reliving (the last thing that a patient wants to face) that it can be known by an other—this time, we hope, an other who will have the courage to participate in the reliving while simultaneously holding the patient's psychological safety as a matter of prime concern. (Bromberg, 2013, p. 191)

and that

> ... in any treatment where trauma is an issue—and I believe trauma to be a factor for every patient in at least some areas of personality—the patient will attempt to talk about the trauma, though always with hidden shame because "talking about" evokes "reliving." The patient, however, will usually reveal enough data to stimulate the therapist's curiosity, setting off a process in which the therapist's accelerated attempt at exploring events for which the patient has no narrative memory leads to an enacted reliving of the trauma, into which the therapist is drawn like a moth to a flame. (Bromberg, 2013, p. 123)

Bromberg is speaking here of trauma as an event. But there is no reason to think things are any different when the trauma is ongoing, repeated daily due to being a member of a stigmatized group. Imagine for a moment living in a body which draws stares, negative comments, judgments. Imagine being seen as ugly, lazy, gluttonous, out of control, ignorant, uneducated, undesirable. Imagine experiencing that every day. Imagine being subjected to these kinds of microaggressions daily.

Like most people, I have tended to think of trauma as something big, events that would cause anyone to suffer long-term effects. But think about what we know from the work done on Repetitive Strain or Stress Injury. It does not take a clearly defined event or injury to produce long lasting problems—poor posture, work that involves repetitive movement over a long period of time, like typing on a keyboard or even knitting can lead to pain and injury to tendons, injury serious enough to warrant surgery, all absent any major event or injury. As we have looked more deeply at development and trauma, we now see that the same is true on the psychic level, that repeated patterns of failure to respond to a child or support development can also lead to trauma absent any major observable failure or specific event. On the psychic level, microaggression is the analog to repetitive strain.

> Microaggressions are the everyday verbal, nonverbal, and environmental slights, snubs, or insults, whether intentional or unintentional, which communicate hostile, derogatory, or negative messages to target persons based solely upon their marginalized group membership. In many cases, these hidden messages may

invalidate the group identity or experiential reality of target persons, demean them on a personal or group level, communicate they are lesser human beings, suggest they do not belong with the majority group, threaten and intimidate, or relegate them to inferior status and treatment. (Sue, 2010, p. 3)

When I was in college, I spent one summer working with inner city African American children. One day I was working with a beautiful little girl who was about eight years old. Her hair was done in cornrows with pretty beads at the ends. As she looked at me I saw her face change from a bright smile to sadness as she reached out to touch my long hair. "You have good hair," she said. Until that moment I had not understood what having kinky hair meant for a black woman, but in that moment I understood that she was telling me that my "good" hair put me in a different category where beauty was possible and her kinky hair consigned her to a group that did not meet the dominant standards for beauty.

Recently Janice Bennett, an African American psychoanalyst, wrote about her experience of living as a member of a stigmatized group:

> The larger world defines me as inferior, a second class citizen placed lower in the racial hierarchy of America where whiteness conveys power, privilege and the right to determine the place of others in the racial caste system. This creates in me a double consciousness or awareness of my place as an American and as an African-American in a world that would deny me my subjectivity.
>
> In addition to the many micro-aggressions I encounter as I traverse the city, the consultation room becomes yet another place where I am traumatized. When I enter the consulting room I feel like I am on trial. The message of my inferior status is alive in the room. I am not sure who the judge and jury are, but I feel I have to prove I am worthy to work not only with all patients, but particularly with those who are white. (Bennett, 2014)

The usually recommended panacea for this, the universal remedy for fat people to deal with this trauma is to lose weight. Lose weight and there will no longer be any of the stares or other negative effects of being fat and the trauma will no longer be present. New research suggests, however, that losing weight does not improve mental health, a finding entirely unexpected by the researcher Sarah Jackson and her colleagues. In their study, they found for fat people who are otherwise healthy and not depressed, at the end of four years the proportion of participants with depressed mood increased by almost 300 percent in the group that lost weight (about fifteen percent of participants) compared to a rather modest eighty-five percent and sixty-two percent increase in mood problems in the weight stable or weight gain groups, respectively. This flies directly in the face of what is commonly believed and in fact what most therapists would believe to be the case. What leads to these findings?

> The poor long-term maintenance of weight loss is notorious, and in itself could be interpreted as demonstrating that the personal costs of losing weight exceed the benefits. Resisting food in environments that offer abundant eating opportunities requires sustained self-control, and given that self-control appears to be a limited resource, other areas of life may suffer as a consequence. Loss of fat stores may also initiate signals for replenishment of adipocytes, thereby stimulating hunger and appetite and making weight control progressively more difficult. These observations suggest that weight loss is a significant psychobiological challenge, and as such, could affect psychological wellbeing. (Jackson, Steptoe, Beeken, Kivimaki, & Wardle, 2014)

Dr. Arya Sharma adds to the authors' conclusions his own caution:

> ... these findings should perhaps caution us against simply advising all overweight or obese people, irrespective of whether or not they actually have weight-related health issues (or are otherwise unhappy with their weight), to try losing some weight. (Sharma, 2011)

Earlier I offered this thought from Donald Kalsched:

> It is different with the victim of early trauma. For these patients, disowned material is not psychically represented, but has been banished to the body or relegated to discrete psychical fragments, between which amnesia barriers have been erected. It must never be allowed to return to consciousness. (Kalsched, 1997, p. 104)

Experiencing repeatedly the kinds of experiences Murray had as she listened to that paper or hearing again and again how unacceptable, ugly, pathological is one's body splits body from mind, body from sense of self as it did for Murray, because it is unbearable to be in a despised and reviled body.

Splitting from the body, dissociating oneself from body as Murray describes is the response to the trauma of being fat, experienced on a daily basis. It is not one that losing weight can solve. How can she embrace and fully inhabit a body that brings her so much pain, shame, and humiliation? Failure to address the split becomes failed treatment no matter how much progress is made in other areas of life. Judging therapy a success because the patient lost weight, as Yalom did, is to spectacularly ignore the split altogether and lay the ground work for further splitting when the weight is regained as it almost inevitably will be.

I wrestled for weeks with what the answer is here, what the solution would be, where healing of this trauma, experienced on a daily basis would come from. Knowing that losing weight does not cure it, I struggled to see how to mend the split, how to keep mind and body together in the face of the very traumatic experiences that repeatedly lead to the split. Then I recalled something Barbara Stevens Sullivan wrote about wounds:

> Patients typically seek a "cure" for their wounds, their anxiety, their obsessions and addictions. Jung denies that "perfection"—which may be thought of as a synonym for "cure"—is possible. My own experience, on both sides of the couch, suggests that even "healing" may be a problematic word. In some sense, a person is her wounds. A sapling, planted beside a supportive stake that the gardener neglects to remove, will grow around the stake. The stake's presence will injure the growing tree; the tree will adapt by distorting its "natural" shape to accommodate the stake. But the mature tree will be the shape it has taken; it cannot be "cured" of the injury, the injury is an intrinsic aspect of its nature. (Stevens Sullivan, 2009, p. 174)

Long though we may to escape this wound, it is a part of us; we have taken the shape that it has given and continues to give us.

I know that we have to return to the split and to find what will bring the parts back together again, to hold them together. It is necessary to return to the body rather than escape into mind. I kept coming back to embodiment but how to accomplish that? Fall Ferguson, president of ASDAH (Association for Size Diversity and Health), posted on the association's blog:

> I define embodiment as a process of paying attention to our experiences that includes our physical experiences—our sensations—as well as any emotions and thoughts that arise in the present moment. Like meditation or relaxation practices, embodiment is a skill that can be cultivated with a variety of different practices. Embodiment practices have for me been an integral part of healing body shame. (Ferguson, 2014)

Embodiment practices and exercises are important tools. Finding images in ourselves and in art that support the fat body—Rubens' nudes, Botero's massive bronzes and his charming and coy paintings of his fat wife. In 1994 Laurie Toby Edison published the first book of fat female nudes, *Women En Large*. Leonard Nimoy photographed nude fat women and published his book, *The Full Body Project*. Both books contain images that show fat women as voluptuous, as desirable, as strong and beautiful. Affirmations of appreciation for our bodies. Massage. Movement. Mindfulness meditation. All of this helps.

For the therapist, there is another dimension to this issue, one more reminiscent of the Fisher King, he of the wound that will not heal, than it is of healing and cure. In Jungian circles we speak of the wounded healer as an archetype behind the therapeutic enterprise. This comes from Jung's important recognition:

> Freud himself accepted my suggestion that every doctor should submit to a training analysis before interesting himself in the unconscious of his patients for therapeutic purposes. ... We could say, without too much exaggeration, that a good half of every treatment that probes at all deeply consists in the doctor's examining himself, for only what he can put right in himself can he hope to put right in the patient. This, and nothing else, is the meaning of the Greek myth of the wounded physician. (Jung, 1966, pp. 115–116)

As therapists we must remain aware of our wounds, which like the Fisher King's do not heal. A wound healed in some ways can become a wound forgotten, a wound sealed over and out of consciousness. Allowing the wound that will not heal to remain in our conscious awareness means not only remembering wounding experiences of the past but, in the case of membership in a stigmatised group, remaining aware of the daily trauma of that membership. It means not splitting, while also not escaping the traumatic experience of the gaze. This is the territory of both/and where I both affirm myself in the body I have and remain aware of the trauma of having a stigmatized body.

Near the end of her piece, Bennett writes:

> My own gaze meets my patient's; our mutual gaze allows both of us to begin to explore the binary that is white patient, black analyst. The task is difficult. The dilemma is being caught in the polarities of white/black, good/evil, and idealization/envy, shame/pride and so on, all of which can limit the freedom of expression for both parties.
>
> The space between these dualities is where the analytic work is done. Delving in to the difficult spaces–the gray areas–happens only when both members of the dyad see each other as full and equal participants in the process. (Bennett, 2014)

Her words bring to mind some by Jung—"The meeting of two personalities is like the contact of two chemical substances: if there is any reaction, both are transformed" (Jung, 1933, p. 49).

In 2012 and 2013, IPTAR, the Institute for Psychoanalytic Training and Research, sponsored conferences—Black Psychoanalysts Speak. One of the panelists, Anton Hart, offers another way that the trauma of a stigmatized identity is overlooked:

> One stereotype about psychoanalysis is that it focuses on you, and what's in you, and your internal conflicts, and holds you responsible for your predicament. One could say blames you for your predicament. If you're a person who's been oppressed, if you're a person who has been discriminated against, then there's a way in which that may implicitly minimize what's been done to you, your trauma. Here's this white guy going to tell me that I'm struggling right now, not because I was discriminated against, for instance, but because of my internal conflict. (Winograd, 2014)

It does not fall only to therapists to hold awareness of the wound but also for anyone working through the trauma of being fat. The wound must be opened and cleaned by expressing the feelings inherent in living with constant scrutiny, judgment, and rejection, in living in a stigmatized body. Expressing the anger, the fear, the sadness. The grief of life not lived, the letting go of the fantasy that one day some thinner inner self will emerge and erase the stigma. All of this needs to be allowed. It means knowing that these are the cards I was dealt and that it falls to me to play them and make of my life something more than the trauma. I am fat, but I am not only fat.

CHAPTER TEN

Back to the consulting room: blind spots and remedies

I n a book about the impact of the personal history and experiences of analysts, Steven Kuchuck wrote:

> Having key elements of oneself labeled pathological, especially by the field you have turned to for healing, professional identity, and development, wreaks havoc with even the most securely formed psyche. (Kuchuck, 2013, p. xx)

Kuchuck was speaking of his treatment as a gay man when he was in training at a psychoanalytic institute, where he was told he should conceal this basic fact of his identity. For someone who is homosexual, disclosure of this aspect of identity is voluntary as there are no visible markers. But disclosure is not optional for the fat person or the person of color. We have no way to "pass," to blend into the cultural background. We are immediately subject to a scrutinizing gaze as soon as we walk into a room. Before we open our mouths, before any questions are asked, regardless of whether we are present as therapist or patient or ordinary person, we are subject to the projections common to the cultural complexes about us. When I first read Kuchuck's statement, tears came as I know very well what he writes. When those two analysts told me that though they believed I would make a good analyst, I would not be accepted because of my weight, I experienced that havoc. How could it be that they or anyone could say that? That they could not just think but say that in one breath both that I would make a good analyst and that my weight disqualified me was dumbfounding. Even now, more than twenty years later, that stings and leaves me somewhat bewildered even as I know they were reflecting the bias that I and every fat person encounters dozens of times each day. I expected more and better of "the field [I] have turned to for healing, professional identity, and development" (Kuchuck, 2013, p. xx). When any of us experiences judgment and/or rejection in a relationship or place where we should reasonably expect care and concern—from a therapist or doctor, from a loved one, within the family—then we experience trauma, the trauma of being judged or rejected for some basic aspect of ourselves.

Blind spots in depth psychology

I have looked at other cultural issues with which analytical psychology has also struggled and continues to struggle to see how and when change happened. Thirty years ago Polly Young Eisendrath wrote about the absence of African-Americans among the ranks of Jungian analysts. She observed:

> As Jungians we hold certain beliefs and ideals about healthy functioning and aspects of personal subjectivity. Our explanatory concepts about personality are weighted in the direction of a universal, autonomous Self ... We have come to believe—to a greater or lesser degree—in this formulation of subjectivity because we have joined with other Jungians and have read and studied with them. We write and speak about individual subjectivity as though it is made up of universal states of being interacting with our conscious experience of subjectivity. (Young Eisendrath, 1987, p. 47)

If being a Jungian analyst means having an analysis with a white analyst, training with white trainees taught by white faculty, then the belief easily arises that what they learn and experience, because it is limited to the white experience, is universally valid. Absent challenge and/or exposure to people of color, how could it be otherwise?

Even knowing about and abhorring racism in the culture at large and believing themselves not to be racist cannot protect against the parochial limitations of the Jungian world, even though it is not by conscious design almost exclusively white.

In some ways it is easier to grapple with racial issues, though not necessarily to do so successfully, because the culture as a whole struggles with it. Indeed the last fifty years have been deeply marked by our efforts to legislate racial equality even as we know lived equality is much harder to achieve. As Young Eisendrath observes, "Racism is a psychological complex organised around the archetype of Opposites, the splitting of experience into Good and Bad, White and Black, Self and Other" (Young Eisendrath, 1987, p. 42). Michel Vannoy Adams commented on her article:

> There remains a conspicuous underrepresentation of African Americans among analysts of all persuasions—and, I would add, among patients. Historically, African Americans have been disenfranchised in many ways, including psychoanalytically ... For psychoanalysis adequately to serve disenfranchised populations, I maintain that it must effectively engage what I call the cultural unconscious. (Adams, 1988, p. 183)

Adams here anticipates the development of Kimbles and Singer's work on the cultural complex and the distance between recognizing what needs to be done and doing it. In the case of the white analyst and the African-American patient, each, whether they want to or not, like to or not, involuntarily discloses this basic part of their identities, that is, the element of identity that is tied to skin color. This seldom happens though, because there are so very few African-American analysands, which tends to keep the cultural complex about race in the closet rather than in the consulting room where it could be put into words which would allow it to become more conscious. In order for analytical psychology to become more diverse, it and psychoanalysis must engage with both African-American culture and with the cultural complexes about race.

Homosexuality is another example of a cultural complex that analytical psychology, and indeed the whole mental health community, has struggled with. It is only since the late 1980s that homosexuality has received much attention in analytical psychology. Robert Hopcke published his article, "Jung and homosexuality: a clearer vision" (Hopcke, 1988a) in the *Journal of Analytical Psychology* in 1988 in which he explored Jung's statements about homosexuality. He showed Jung to have written five different attitudes toward homosexuality and advanced three different theories of its etiology. In his book, *Jung, Jungians and Homosexuality*, published in 1989, he further suggests that "Jung viewed homosexuality as a form of immaturity caused, in part, by a disturbance of the relationship with the parents, particularly the mother" (Hopcke, 1988, p. 73). Until the 1970s, homosexuality was considered on its face pathological and it was not until 1987 that it was fully removed from the *Diagnostic and Statistical Manual* (DSM) as a diagnosable condition. Although today, as the movement for LGBT rights and marriage equality gains success, still there remain attempts to explain homosexual orientation, which, as Rubin suggested, implicitly carry the assumption that it is in some way problematic. In contrast, heterosexuality, which is what is termed an "unmarked category" assumed to be normal, is not seen as problematic and rarely if ever are there attempts to explain it.

Eugene Monick, also writing in the late 80s asserts, "The effort to dictate who a man should love is perverted theology. It is the psychological counterpart of monotheism, dominated by patriarchal triumphalism, demanding adherence to the patriarch's one true god" (Monick, 1987, p. 120). More recently Withers writes, "Heterosexual (and analytic) assumptions about what constitutes good (healthy, object-related) loving relationships are culturally, not psychologically, determined and homosexual culture may be different from heterosexual culture" (Withers, 2003, p. 161). In the debates about what homosexuality is, what causes it and all the rest of the debates surrounding it, we see again the presence of a cultural complex. Barry Miller writes:

> What was previously considered a sexual behaviour has become a psychological identity; what was something that a person did has become who they are. This is a subtle, but significant shift in the perception of the "Other" and of oneself …
>
> Is homosexuality a choice, a pathological condition, a natural variety, the result of genetic alteration, pre-natal hormonal influence, maternal disturbance or paternal neglect? Is it perversion, subversion, regression, resistance, or the result of a "possession?" Where we find ourselves in this struggle to define it is based

primarily on the dominant value orientations we carry, orientations that may even be outside our own awareness. How we approach the very subject of homosexuality and its implications comes out of our alignment with psychological, theological, and political identifications. We look at this subject through thick lenses with extensive histories of all sorts. (B. Miller, 2010, p. 113)

I maintain that what Miller says about homosexuality applies equally well to fat. Is it not also true that fat is seen as;

a choice, a pathological condition, a natural variety, the result of genetic alteration, pre-natal hormonal influence, maternal disturbance or paternal neglect? Is it perversion, subversion, regression, resistance, or the result of a "possession?" … How we approach the very subject of [obesity] and its implications comes out of our alignment with psychological, theological, and political identifications. We look at this subject through thick lenses with extensive histories of all sorts.

It seems appropriate here to repeat what Rubin said: "The search for a cause is a search for something that could change so that these 'problematic' [phenomena] would simply not occur"(Saguy, 2012, p. 70). In other words, the assumption is that a cause once found will allow this phenomenon to no longer exist, that implicitly it would be better if homosexuality were eliminated. The search for cause implies a need, a wish, a desire to change the person in some basic way. Miller challenges this project: "Clearly the individuation promoted in analysis is not to change the homosexual to a heterosexual, and not to make the promiscuous man monogamous. If change is not the goal, then what might be expected?" (B. Miller, 2010, p. 122). Is not the goal of analysis that a person becomes more fully himself or herself, regardless of the desires and agenda of the analyst? When the analyst has an agenda, and image of how her patient should be, should look, should live, can that analyst really claim to be serving that analytic goal of individuation? Do we want the African American to become white, the gay person straight as well as the fat person thin?

It often seems that the normative Jungian analyst is a heterosexual slender white male, despite the reality that female analysts outnumber the males. It does seem to be the male lens through which so much of analytical psychology continues to view the world. Though he speaks to the issue of the paucity of African-American patients and analysts, Adams offers:

> It is not enough for an analyst, especially one who is not a member of the same ethnic group as the dreamer, merely to have an empathic and sensitive attitude. Ideally, what such a case requires is an analyst with substantial knowledge of the specific cultural unconscious germane to the case. An analyst who is a member of a different ethnic group will not, of course, have had the same cultural experience as the dreamer. Such an analyst may, however, even in the absence of that experience, acquire considerable knowledge of the cultural unconscious of the ethnic group of which the dreamer is a member. No analytic institutes with which I am familiar, whether they be in the Freudian tradition or the Jungian tradition, offer courses in the content of specific contemporary cultures. (Adams, 1988, p. 193)

The African-American patient, the LGBT patient, the fat patient all have every reason to want and expect the analyst to go beyond expectable empathy to developing more awareness of cultural complexes and the blindness that these complexes bring. White privilege, straight privilege, and thin privilege shape the view and experience of their beneficiaries a great deal more than even the most enlightened imagine. It is the influence of privilege and cultural complexes that these three issues in analytical psychology have in common.

Is the cultural fat complex all that is at play in the silence in the Jungian literature about fat and more specifically responding to the fat person? Em Farrell, a British psychotherapist suggests, "I suspect the hardest thing to do about obesity is to stop and think about it." (Farrell, n.d.). Indeed there is very little evidence of thought about the experience of being fat, what that experience of being fat and living in a fat body means, or the effect of the presence of a fat person on a slender person and vice versa. Given the absence of fat voices in discourse about fat, it is no wonder there is so little thought here.

The body in analysis

Analytical psychology and psychoanalysis both have a history of ignoring the body, especially women's bodies fat or thin. The avoidance of the body is known and written about by a number of Jungians, among them Marion Woodman, Anita Greene, Gottfried Heuer, all of whom incorporate body work of various kinds into their analytic practices. But as Heuer notes, "Jungian psychology seems marked by a theoretical ambivalence towards the body, whilst mostly ignoring it clinically … so the post-Jungians have only rarely engaged with the body in their theoretical and clinical work" (Heuer, 2012, p. 12).

Other than a few pieces by Polly Young Eisendrath, Clarissa Pinkola Estes, and Marion Woodman, there is very little in the Jungian literature where we can find discussion of the female body from the perspective of actual women. Of the many effects on women's lives and bodies of the stages of the reproductive cycle. Of the pregnant body. Of the deviant body. Of the mutilated body. Of the objectification of the female body and the fruitless quest for perfection that occupies the lives of so many girls and women. Of the aging body. Where are women's voices about women's bodies and psyches? Yet without a body, we become like the nymph Echo, a voice without body condemned to echo what she hears rather than speak her own experience.

Rosemary Balsam, a psychoanalyst, took up this problem of the absence of the female body in psychoanalysis in her book, *Women's Bodies in Psychoanalysis*. She begins by asking,

> How do we talk about bodies? How do we think about our analysands' bodies? How do we contemplate our own bodily presence in the office? How can we think more about our own bodies in relation to our patients? And those messages from past bodily experience that the mind holds in its "jar"—how do we render them to another person to increase their comprehensibility? (Balsam, 2012, p. 1)

Such important questions and so little discussed. We all have bodies. In every consulting room, body meets body. So why the silence about the body, especially the female body?

Both Balsam and Heuer contemplate this problem of silence. Heuer suggests:

> … body became Shadow because it renders us powerless vis-à-vis the vicissitudes of desire, ageing and death, and so was split off from the more valued mental and spiritual aspects of human experience. Thus excluded, that which is not valued becomes evil.

This bias continues to flourish in analysis: in clinical practice the predominant aim is to touch the soul, never the body. Yet it is the body that constitutes our being in the world as matter, in that it forms the very basis from which we relate and interact with ourselves, with others and with the spiritual dimension of being. (Heuer, 2012, p. 2)

Like Jung, Heuer sees body as shadow, avoided because it inevitably brings into the room those aspects of life we most wish to avoid—death, aging, desire, greed, excess. Certainly the fat body, and especially the fat female body carries this shadow and inevitably activates in both patient and analyst all of the anxieties attendant upon these shut off aspects of life.

Balsam sees another reason for avoidance:

The silence in psychoanalysis about the female body—whether it is the patient's or the analyst's, and whether it manifests itself in a theory, in treatment, in a fin de siècle hysteria, or in a contemporary clinical presentation—suggests that this is yet another venue in which the internal and external aspects of bodily experience have not yet been integrated. Despite our clinical sophistication, it is difficult to sustain a mental integration of body and mind. How humanly eager we all are—analysand and analyst alike—to seek the transient but seductive comfort of dwelling with less anxiety in the mental spaces of splits, schisms, and rifts, where physical explanations and mental ones are kept in separate compartments. (Balsam, 2012, p. 8)

We stay where we, both therapist and patient, can maintain the split of body from mind, where we can both see the body as something handy for transporting the head and the all important mind.

Earlier I somewhat jokingly speculated that the normative Jungian analyst is a slender white heterosexual male. Assuming for the sake of argument that this is true at least so far as determining the issues that analytical psychology concerns itself with, how does this relate to silence about the body?

In 1975, Laura Mulvey published a paper in which she identifies for the first time what she called "the male gaze" which she asserts is the film industry's assumption that the movie spectator is a man. Mulvey describes it this way:

> In a world ordered by sexual imbalance, pleasure in looking has been split between active/male and passive/female. The determining male gaze projects its phantasy on to the female form which is styled accordingly. (Mulvey, 1975)

Sharon Green draws from Mulvey and extends her insight:

> Through this gaze (which is active), the woman is seen only as an erotic (passive) object signifying patriarchal male fantasies about the female body and feminine identity. The norms of physical beauty and gender performance to which the woman is expected to aspire and comply are created and maintained through these fantasies. (Green, 2010, p. 344)

An important, if not the most important factor in the belief that the fat woman should lose weight arises from the male gaze. And for analysands, this is true whether the analyst is male or female as female analysts also operate under the male gaze and thus take on, unconsciously, the imperative for a woman to be attractive, the parameters for attractive being determined by that gaze. Recall what Yalom said of his patient Betty, as quoted in Chapter 3. He does not even question that she or any patient should be expected to meet his standard of attractiveness in a woman. Male privilege affords to him the assumption that attractive means what is attractive to men. "How dare they impose that body on the rest of us?" Isn't that what the whole War on Obesity is all about? How dare we impose our too-muchness on the rest of you, on the slender world? Is it any wonder that male privilege enters the consulting room?

Sharon Green says of the objectifying male gaze:

> I am going to retain that term to emphasize the historical milieu in which I grew up—a world in which all spectators were assumed to be adult men, all pronouns masculine, where the God of my family and church could only be imagined to be a masculine entity, and where "the" masculine was conflated with activity and subjectivity, and "the" feminine with passivity and objectification. (Green, 2010, p. 345)

Analytical psychology is rife with these gendered assumptions, which are often vigorously defended even by women.

Jung wrote in 1927:

> But who, if it comes to that, has fully realized that history is not contained in thick books but lives in our very blood? So long as a woman lives the life of the past she can never come into conflict with history. But no sooner does she begin to deviate, however slightly, from a cultural trend that has dominated the past than she encounters the full weight of historical inertia, and this unexpected shock may injure her, perhaps fatally. (Jung, 1970, p. 130)

Something that is still all too true today. Deviating from the cultural norm gets one tagged as pathological. In the West it is no longer the case that a woman is expected to eschew ambition and stay at home raising children and caring for the home; that cultural trend has faded away for the most part. But it is still expected that a woman conform to the image of ideal femininity, that is be slender and visually appealing to men. As Balsam, writing in 2012, says: "The environment of male domination in a phallocentric society makes it psychologically important for women themselves to be internally silent, consolidating superego prohibitions against public or interpersonal discourse about their bodies." (Balsam, 2012, p. 10).

We see there is an unease with the body in general as it brings shadow and the specter of ageing, illness, death, greed with it into the room. And women's bodies in particular carry the additional burden of the demands of the patriarchal male gaze. As Young Eisendrath puts it:

> … female beauty dominates the lives of women and men through the formula that female beauty equals power. Wherever I am and whoever I'm with, I overhear evaluative comments about female appearances … Both women and men evaluate women according to the shapes and sizes of their faces, legs, hips, and breasts. As a psychotherapist and a feminist, I frequently feel helpless to break the link between female appearance and power. (Young Eisendrath, 2012, p. 82)

I think back to the analyst I met for tea that summer morning several years ago and to what those two analysts told me about my weight and my desire to become an analyst and I remember what Eugene Monick said of homosexuality: "The effort to dictate who a man should love is perverted theology. It is the psychological counterpart of monotheism, dominated by patriarchal triumphalism, demanding adherence to the patriarch's one true god"(Monick, 1987, p. 120). Is that not also true of bodies? Is not the demand that, at the very least, the effort be made for all bodies to be slender also "the psychological counterpart of monotheism, dominated by patriarchal triumphalism, demanding adherence to the patriarch's one true god"?

Wilchins asks:

> What kind of system bids us each make of our bodies a problem to be solved, a claim we must defend, or a secret we must publicly confess, again and again? [...] The question really should be [...] whose agenda is it that demands your hips must be gendered with a particular meaning or to even have any meaning at all? (Wilchins, 1997, p. 39)

Balsam's work makes it quite clear that psychoanalysis needs to deal with the issue of the woman's body, to bring women's bodies and attendant issues into the consulting room. And it is clear that the depth psychologies tend to avoid issues of body, whether male or female. Balsam beautifully states the vital importance of body in the work of analysis:

> All of us have bodies; we can see them, recognize their outlines; touch them, smell them even. We can tell our own bodies apart from other people, at the same time that we know that we are more alike than different. We all eat, extracting in a complicated fashion from the world around us the life-giving elements that we need, and eliminating the waste of that process. We have skin, nerves, blood vessels, and muscle and organ sensations; we walk, talk, see, and hear. We feel pleasure, anger, fear, and pain. We cry. We live cooperatively or we war, or are isolated. All born of females ... whether we like it or not, we are identified by our genitals as male or female in almost every culture on the globe. We mature as sexual beings. We choose mates; most of us procreate and take care of our young. Once young ourselves, we grow older. Our organs fail; we die. The next generation takes over and mourns loss. All of this raw

physicality, with its average-expectable patterning as we live and observe it over the span of our lives, exists somewhere within us. It contributes richly to our private thinking, and serves as a backdrop to all of our interactive dealings with others. (Balsam, 2012, p. 2)

Who can read that and not feel its truth? Yet, our problem remains. As Janet Tintner says, "even with the best of intentions, it is very hard, as an analyst, to pursue a line of inquiry that touches on issues that are personally painful" (Tintner, 2010, p. 289).

Remedies

What is the work that remains? In order for issues of the body to come into the consulting room, therapists have to become comfortable with their own bodies and the issues with and about body that patients bring. That is a starting place. And we need to do the work to become conscious of the cultural fat complex that so dominates the discourse on fat and health and women's bodies, both in and out of the consulting room. And there is more, as Thomas Singer indicates:

> The fate of the world does not in fact hinge on the thread of the individual psyche. Rather, the emergence of a theory of cultural complexes suggests that an understanding of the individual psyche through its consciousness will not be enough. The group itself will need to develop a consciousness of its cultural complexes. Perhaps each injured culture—be it Balkan, American, Black, White, Palestinian, Israeli, Iraqi, Catholic, Jewish, Jungian, Freudian, men, women (the list is endless once you begin to think in terms of cultural complexes)—needs to learn how to drink to the dregs its own complexes, as well as those of its neighbors, allies and enemies. To settle down the archetypal defenses of the group spirit, the collective psyche itself and its often traumatized, sometimes immature or stunted, spirit needs to individuate, and this is not the work of an individual alone or of analysis alone. (Singer, 2004, pp. 31–32)

Both the dominant group and the injured group need "to learn how to drink to the dregs its own complexes, as well as those of its neighbors, allies and enemies."

Looking within

Earlier I stated that it is usually assumed that in a room with a slender therapist and a fat patient, it is the patient who has a weight problem. That therapist, benefitting from thin privilege may well assume that the way she eats, what she eats and how she exercises are what make her different from her patient, what make her thin and her patient fat. She may believe that because she carefully monitors what she eats and faithfully exercises, that she has control over her body, control that the fat woman could have if only she tried harder and did as she does. There is nothing in the media or even the professional literature to contradict her assumptions.

There are powerful transference/countertransference forces operating in therapy when fat enters the picture. As a fat patient I came to work with slender analysts with a full set of baggage and expectations based solely on my fears and projections about how my fat body would be experienced and regarded. Nothing in my experience with others contradicted these fears, and more often than not, my fears were borne out as valid. The language used to describe obesity—words like "grotesque," "gargantuan," "repulsive"—betray much about feelings toward fat people. It is important for the slender therapist to look within about her own attitudes and responses to fat. As Drell wrote:

> In examining one's countertransference responses to obese patients in psychotherapy, it is important to note that the obese patient's appearance may actually be repulsive, distorting the human physique to grotesque proportions ... Therapists should intermittently ask themselves how they feel about their patients' obesity and how they have minimized or exaggerated the meaning of the patients' excess weight. If in the course of therapy, the patients' obesity is to be discussed or if it is discussed to the exclusion of other issues, therapists should examine their countertransference responses as well as the patients' resistances. (Drell, 1988, p. 79)

A fat patient who wants to talk about weight exclusively, as if it were all that matters in life, is as much avoidant as is the fat patient who ignores weight entirely. Furthermore, in either case, the therapist needs to be aware of how her own biases and/or discomfort play a role in this.

There are very fine lines here. Weight and appearance and being outside the established norms are touchy things. It is difficult to become accepting of one's own deviant body, to be at home with being different. The ambivalence is massive. The longing to fit in is right there next to defiance and anger about not being accepted. The therapist needs to walk that line without falling to either side, either by urging and cajoling weight loss or by denying the difficulties of being, as Gutwill put it, "freakish." These are tricky waters for a therapist with thin privilege to try to navigate.

Just as Michael Vannoy Adams said that white analysts need to learn about African-American culture, our fictional slender analyst needs to learn about the life her fat patient leads, about fat experience, about the experience of being reviled, judged, shunned, pathologised on a daily basis. And consider what her own unresolved body issues might be, because as Barbara Miller writes:

> the experience of the analyst may … have to do with his or her own neurotic blind spots. And the analyst needs to consider such a possibility. Concerning neurosis Jung writes, "Behind a neurosis there is often concealed all the natural and necessary suffering the patient has been unwilling to bear" … And we can say that the analyst's own not suffered pain can all too easily be disowned and then "found" as the pain of the analysand: the neurotic counter-transference. (B. H. Miller, 2010, p. 154)

A female therapist, regardless of her weight, has had to deal with the expectations that women should be slender and attractive. Most likely she has dieted or thought about dieting, fretted about any fluctuation in her weight, and experienced some anxiety about whether or not she is pretty enough, slender enough to attract a partner. In this sense she and her fat patient have shared experience, but her patient's anxiety and fretting have not resulted in the slender body that the therapist has. And this can well become a source for a blind spot in the therapist—if she has been able through diet and exercise to be thin, then why wouldn't that also be the answer for her fat patient.

That slender therapist needs to consider where her ideas about fat and fat people come from, what supports those ideas. When I started college in 1964, Duke University had been integrated for just one year. I was shocked when one of my dorm mates, a young woman from

Mississippi, stated as a matter of fact that the skin of African Americans felt different, had a different texture from that of white people. For her, moving up north to Duke was as big a change in terms of racial exposure as mine was moving south. Both of us moved outside of our culture into one where norms were different and changing. Her statement was racist, yes, but also thoroughly consistent with the norms and values of the culture in which she had been raised. It was shocking to me because it differed so from my culture, which, because I was an "Army brat" had always been racially diverse and integrated. Her racism, though appalling, is not significantly different from the anti-fat bias which assumes fat people are gluttons, lazy, and undisciplined. That sole article in Quadrant in which obesity is even addressed carries this bias right in the keywords given for the article: obesity, gorging, overeating, gluttony, hunger.

Outside of the realm of fat studies, the Health At Every Size movement, and fat acceptance circles, the fat person is not seen as trustworthy or reliable about her own lived experience because it is assumed she is always defensive and denying the reality of her condition. If she says she eats moderately, often it will be asserted that she is in denial about how much she actually eats or some comment will be made about the unreliability of self-report. The fat woman is simply not trustworthy.

In five years of research I could find only two articles written by fat therapists about their experiences of being fat–articles by Jane Burka and Janet Tintner, both of whom I mention. A third appeared very recently with the publication in *Psychoanalytic Inquiry* of "What's fat got to do with it? On different kinds of losses and gains in the analytic relationship" by Caryn Sherman-Meyer. Surely there are more of us who could contribute to this necessary conversation. Some of the most important books coming out of fat studies and the effort to counter the dominant narrative were written not by fat people, but by thin people who, by virtue of being thin, were given credibility. Paul Campos, Abigail Saguy, Linda Bacon come immediately to mind and all three carry thin privilege and acknowledge that. Would their books have gotten the recognition they have had they been written by fat people? I doubt it. Becoming aware of thin privilege is an important step in doing the work that remains.

Returning to Bion's dictum to approach each session without memory or desire is critical in order to resolve the cultural fat complex. If the therapist has in mind that her fat patient needs to lose weight in order to heal, whatever that means, then she is in fact imposing her agenda without determining if that is what the patient wants or needs. Laura Bogart offers a stunning example of this in a piece she wrote for Salon:

> My therapist is a petite woman with opinions as sharp as her suits. She has told me that she will stop treating me if I don't begin a weight loss program. I am 23 at the time, and I don't know that I can say no to her. She's wept when I've shared stories of my father's rages; she's asked to see my scars. And she says that, by not forcing me to confront this horrible hindrance that is my body, she is "enabling" me, allowing me to deny myself my brightest, happiest life. (Bogart, 2013)

When the therapist holds this desire for her patient to change in particular ways, when she asserts her own agenda for the patient, Sullivan suggests that desire "reflects a yearning to be helped. 'If I can put all the woundedness I sense in the room into the patient, and if I can fix it in him, I will be fixed, too'" (Stevens Sullivan, 2009, p. 195).

The assumption, for both therapist and patient, most often is that if the patient loses weight and becomes slender, she will become more the person she is meant to be, that she will be healthier and happier. Sharrell Luckett, an actor, writer, and scholar, explores this in her article, "YoungGiftedandFat: performing transweight identities." In her experience of moving from fat to thin, she discovered something quite unexpected:

> So what occurs when the fat black female performing body transforms to slender and then engages in the performance of "thin-ness"? What happens when the black female body physically "passes" in a new way? What happens when a formerly fat, black body experiences "double consciousness" in a historically new way: a way in which how the "other" sees the body affords that body a privilege that is unfamiliar, abounding with humanistic perks …
>
> When I crossed the border, not only was my physical body altered, but my psychological state was significantly affected as well. I changed physically and mentally in ways that I am aware of and ways that I am still discovering. I transformed from physically inferior to physically elite, from ugly to attractive, and from undesirable to desirable. My body now reads as happy, healthy, and worthy of protection. As an actress I went from mammy to mother

(or wife), and from asexual, ensemble roles to sexy leading roles. I
went from my body being fully costumed to scantily clad. My new
body serves as a document of acceptance, my "passport," if you
will, into a new privileged location. At near starvation, I crossed
the border that allowed me to immigrate into an ideal American
size. However, *I'm just as morbidly obese mentally as I was morbidly
obese physically five years ago. My outer appearance morphed, but my
psyche remained the same.* I do not believe myself to be a slender
woman, so I feel as though I'm performing slenderness and femininity in life or in the virtual reality of the stage. As I experience
fat and thin, unprivileged and privileged separately, I purposefully
create and write towards a desegregation of identity. (Luckett, 2014)
(Emphasis added)

Being fat goes beyond the amount of flesh on the body frame. In the
performance text that she wrote from her experience, Luckett describes
three characters now inhabiting her:

My story is told through the voice of my fat identity (Fat), my
slender identity (Skinny), and my liminal identity (Sharrell). "Fat"
often speaks from the past, when she lived in the fat body, but
Fat recognizes that she is trapped in a slender, unfamiliar body.
"Skinny," who lives and experiences the world in a slender body, is
a purposefully under-developed character because she is relatively
young, existing only a little over four years. "Sharrell" is the
character who straddles the border. She represents the fat psyche
coupled with the premature slender psyche who both live in the
slender body. (Luckett, 2014)

For any fat woman, her fat identity will remain no matter her weight—
her memories of being fat, of her longings and pain alongside secret
delight in her big body—are part of the fabric of her being and need to
be heard, witnessed, and accepted. For the thin therapist this may mean
receiving anger toward her as a representative of thin privilege, as one
of the oppressors her fat patient has lived with. I think of my own rage
when my first analyst blithely suggested I could lose a few pounds no
matter my goals. A paradox for the therapist of a fat patient is that as
Sullivan says, "the analyst must let go of desire, even the desire to help,
at the same time as she remains involved and concerned, desiring the

best for her patient" (Stevens Sullivan, 2009, p. 242) and, I would add, accept that the best for her patient may not be what she herself would want or choose.

Fat acceptance and fat culture

The fat acceptance movement grew out of various identity politics movements in the 1960s. It has come to include advocacy groups, fashion and arts events, shopping, swimming, and other sports clubs. In short it has become its own culture in much the same way that gay culture has emerged from gay identity politics.

It is not difficult to access the world of fat acceptance. There are dozens of blogs. Fat studies is an emerging academic field with its own journal, conferences, and a growing number of books are available examining the issues of what I am calling a fat cultural complex. But in order to access that world, the thin person must be willing to grant to fat people the status of reliable reporters, as trustworthy observers and narrators of our own experience.

Unlike the LGBT communities, there is no geographic fat community so it mostly is to be found online. Unlike the earlier days of the movement for LGBT rights, where concentrations of gay people could be found in most cities, fat people are distributed throughout the culture in every socio-economic group. The most common groups catering to fat people actually serve to reinforce the social stricture against being fat—groups like Weight Watchers and Overeaters Anonymous exist to enforce the dominant paradigm, not to empower fat people to claim their own goals and desires. As Farrell suggests:

> Frantz Fanon talked of the internalised racist where the ideology of whites was internalised by Blacks. So that Blacks too associated being Black with failing, being lazy, being less, being stupid and being white meant having power, being successful and being pure! The black man or woman idealised the system of white hierarchy and held it in their own mind as a model. The same is true for people who believe themselves to be fat. They believe the propaganda that thin is better, not only in terms of health, but that is will make them a better and happier person with a higher status and so they hate who they are. (Farrell, n.d.)

Coming to a place where she can see her body as something other than despised most often must precede being able to see and take on the cultural complex. There are no fat bars, no resorts where fat people gather in large numbers. Fat people do not have a Provincetown where we can unselfconsciously walk about and be on the beach. This makes the development of community difficult and thus plays a large part in the failure thus far for fat people to have had our "Stonewall moment" and rise up as the gay community did in 1969. The internet has been the catalyst for development of virtual communities where fat people can talk with each other, share experiences and break their isolation. Much of the community clusters around blogs and forms out of the interaction of bloggers with commenters. In these communities, stories of problems with doctors and other health professionals, of insults and bullying, of shame-inducing experiences can be shared among people who have had similar experiences and who can hear the stories without judgment.

While it is inarguable that the development of online communities of fat people, mostly women, is of huge benefit in terms of empowering members to question the dominant discourse around fat, to begin to embrace their own bodies and in the process lose some of the shame of being fat, it is also true that they often foster an "us *vs.* them" mentality. It is important to gain knowledge about what is and is not true about fat, health, weight, and mortality. To embrace civil rights, too often denied fat people. To come to understand that the failure to achieve and maintain significant weight loss is not a mark of weakness and personal failing. To choose to defang the word "fat" and to stop apologizing for taking up space. There is no doubt that all of these things are important and valuable. But along side them, in many fat acceptance communities there develops a rigid anti-dieting stance, an intolerance of any member who continues to express a desire to lose weight or who expresses ambivalence about her fat body. In doing so, the shadow side of the fat complex gets exposed. The desire for thinness becomes as reviled as fatness is in the dominant culture. That desire becomes a shadow in the fat acceptance community and often must go underground to avoid risk of condemnation.

It is easy as a member of what Singer and Kimbles call the injured group to be angry with the dominant group. It is cathartic to express that anger, to call out the prejudice, even to try to make someone benefitting from thin privilege to feel guilty about his or her privilege. It is satisfying to point out again and again the weakness of the support for the bigotry shown to fat people, to claim the moral high ground and feel righteous. But remember that Singer not only said that the dominant culture needs to become conscious of its complexes, but also the injured group "needs to learn how to drink to the dregs its own complexes, as well as those of its neighbors, allies and enemies." That is not so easy.

Weight loss surgery comes in for particular disapproval in fat acceptance communities. There is much to be questioned about the wisdom, the claims, and the motivation for the weight loss surgery industry. And that questioning needs to be done. But when fat people seeking bariatric surgery speak up in many of these fat acceptance communities, acceptance flies out the window to be replaced by shunning and vilification. Zoë C. Meleo-Erwin examines what happened in two of these communities when two well-known fat activists posted publicly on blogs about their decisions to undergo bariatric surgery. In her article, "'A beautiful show of strength': Weight loss and the fat activist self" (Meleo-Erwin, 2011), she details the fallout and debate that followed these disclosures. The debate centered around how far the principle of body autonomy, so fervently advocated in the fat acceptance community when it is about accepting the fat body is challenged. The community had to struggle, and struggles still, with stretching the limits of acceptance to include those who for reasons of health, be it physical or mental, feel they must opt for surgery and lose weight. Even so contained within the debate is the demand that people opting for surgery do so for good reasons, even if the community may not agree that there are good reasons. It becomes a case then of hate the sin, love the sinner which is one step toward confronting the shadow of the fat complex, but only one step.

As a fat therapist I have had to reflect a great deal on these issues. Coming to accept my own body has been a long journey, begun in my early thirties and even today, almost forty years later I stumble onto pockets of the old feelings of shame. Fat acceptance has made my life much better, helped me to be much happier. But I have had to spend time in examining my own attitudes toward weight loss and work in order to be mindful to be as weight neutral with my patients as I am able to be.

Janet Tintner, one of the very few therapists to write about her personal experience with weight, talks about what happened as she first lost, then regained weight:

I knew that patients would see my body altering. Over ninety pounds is obvious. Maybe some patients could miss it, but not all or even most of them. However, there were no overt references to my weight gain amongst my patients. (Tintner, 2010, p. 282)

When her patients talked about weight or made references to weight, she knew she should discuss how they felt about her, about her weight, but she could not. I recognize this, as for a long time, my patients seemed not to notice my weight at all. We colluded in denial of the reality of our bodies. But then the analyst with whom I was doing supervision asked me about this and rather directly suggested that I had to find a way to bring my body into the room. At the time, I nearly always had at least one anorexic patient in my practice. I thought a lot about what it must be like for them to sit across from me and look at my fat body. There I was, their nightmare in the flesh. I remember clearly the first time I was able to approach this issue, to let my patient know we could talk about how she felt about my body, about my weight. My heart pounded and my hands were like ice when I did it the first time. To my great relief, both my patient and I survived and we went on to do good work together. But until I could bring my body into the room, her body also remained outside.

Tintner goes on:

> Obviously, if I could not acknowledge my size, how could my patients discuss their mixed feelings regarding their own bodies? I did not think this through clearly then, but I did learn enough to change my practice. I realized that, with certain patients, I would have to acknowledge that I was overweight. (Tintner, 2010, p. 283)

She decides to have bariatric surgery because she wants greater certainty that she will not lose and then regain the weight:

> In my clinical work, it was important for me that the band increased my odds of maintaining the weight loss. I could finally hope not to repeat the dreaded humiliating experience of my patients witnessing my struggle before their very eyes. This made it easier—for me. If my odds of staying at a stable size improved, I was more willing to consider inviting patients to verbalize their perceptions. (Tintner, 2010, p. 283)

It was only when she lost weight that she began to be able to broach the topic of her body and the visible changes with her patients. She writes that she regrets not having felt able to deal with this issue when she was gaining weight or when she was fat, but she doesn't seem to fully recognize that this remains a problem in the background because on some level she still only feels comfortable dealing with the matter of her body and her patients' responses to and fantasies about it and her weight so long as she is slender. Put in Luckett's terms, it is only her Skinny self who is comfortable with matters of weight. Her Fat self is still ashamed and anxious about talking about her body and weight.

I have to become as comfortable as I can imagine being dealing with issues of body and weight with my patients. But this issue of being weight neutral makes me deal with just what body acceptance and autonomy actually mean. I have to hold my knowledge about the failure rate of weight loss methods of all kinds and not use that knowledge to assert an agenda on my patients. If I actively discourage weight loss in whatever clever way I find, I am no different from the legions of therapists who push weight loss as the path to happiness. In either case, the need and desire of the patient may well be lost in the need and beliefs of the therapist. I can raise relevant questions like "In what way would your life be different if you lost weight?" or explore with her what fat means for her. We can meaningfully explore how she can work on feeling at home in her body, embrace her body as herself rather than something separate from her self without having to advocate or discourage either weight acceptance or weight loss. This is challenging. I have to be aware of my own feelings about having tried to lose weight only to regain it, about the struggles I have had to accept my body, and watch for how they affect how I respond to my patient's issues and feelings. And add into the mix how she sees and what she feels about my body. It can be easy to lose one's bearings.

Jung tells us:

> For two personalities to meet is like mixing two different chemical substances; if there is any combination at all, both are transformed. In any effective psychological treatment the doctor is bound to influence the patient; but this influence can only take place if the patient has a reciprocal influence on the doctor. (…) It is futile for the doctor to shield himself from the influence of the patient and to

surround himself with a smoke-screen of fatherly and professional authority. (Jung, 1966, p. 71)

Practical considerations

Thin privilege can blind therapists to simple practical matters like how the office is furnished. Is the seating wide enough to accommodate a fat body? Is there a chair without arms as an alternative?

What of the patient who comes to therapy specifically wanting help in losing weight?

There is a dilemma here for both the fat therapist and the thin therapist. The thin therapist needs to be well informed about how dismal the success rates for losing significant weight and maintaining that loss are. And ask herself if it is ethical to advocate and support a treatment that is almost certain to fail. Furthermore, what really does she know about losing weight if she herself has never tried? If therapy is about putting feelings into words and about becoming more conscious and aware of the meaning of something like weight and appearance, is a specific goal of weight loss one that a depth psychotherapist should be taking on or advocating?

Drell touches on the pitfalls:

> Patients who seek help in losing weight and then frustrate the therapist by binging or gaining weight produce a direct negative countertransference. The feelings of hopelessness and despair in patients who have started to regain weight may evoke the complementary countertransference responses of anger, helplessness, and ineffectiveness in the therapist. (Drell, 1988, p. 81)

Or consider the fat therapist who herself has ongoing issues with her own weight—feelings of envy easily arise with a patient who manages to lose weight when she herself has failed. Gutwill accurately points out,

> Patient and therapist are both in a transference relationship to the same "culture home" or "culture parent". Although this social home is characterised by class, race, and ethnic hierarchies ... the subject under investigation is the ideal image of women. (Gutwill, 1994, p. 146)

It is a minefield all the way around. Navigating it requires that the therapist be as aware and mindful of her own issues with weight and appearance as possible. There is no research demonstrating therapy as an effective means of attaining and maintaining significant weight loss, just as there is no means with more than a meager success rate for such a goal. For both fat and thin therapists, the more ethical stance, the more analytic stance is to remain neutral on the subject of weight and to consider instead feelings about weight and what weight and appearance mean for our patients.

CHAPTER ELEVEN

Coming out as fat

An important part of resolving the personal fat complex is to embrace my own fat body, to come out as fat. It is a little strange to think about coming out as fat when anyone who sees me knows. It's not like I could hide what I am and pretend to be thin; I cannot escape being fat, not in anyone's wildest imagination, unless of course I am in a room full of blind people.

> Unlike the gay body, the fat body is always already out. The fat body is of course hypervisible in terms of its mass in relation to the thinner bodies that surround it. As Moon suggests, the fat body displays "a stigma that could never be hidden because it simply is the stigma of visibility", and asks the question "What kind of secret can the body of the fat woman keep?" (Murray, 2005a, p. 153)

No matter what I do, no matter what my accomplishments, no matter how charming I am or intelligent or engaging or interesting, no matter what, I am fat. That cannot be hidden or escaped.

Working on a project like this often has interesting side effects. I started this six years ago just after the actor/director Kevin Smith was asked to leave a Southwest Airlines plane because he refused to buy a second seat and they deemed him too fat to fly. I had never considered that a person could actually be made to leave a commercial airliner because he or she was too fat. So what happened to Smith made me angry and feel compelled to begin to write and be more public about my life as a fat person. I first wrote about coming out as fat that summer. But since then, as I have read, thought, and written about fat, I have arrived at a more nuanced stance about what coming out fat is and what it is not. I have made a place for the ambivalence that has been there unacknowledged for me all along.

According to Goffman, being fat is a form of stigmatized identity and that people with stigmatized identities use three types of identity management: passing, covering, and withdrawing. (Goffman, 1963). There really is no way for me to pass as "normal"; my body carries and reveals my difference immediately. And Luckett's example suggests that even when a fat person becomes thin, that fat stigmatized identity remains alive in the psyche. She describes a kind of passing that can be utilised by that small fraction of successful dieters. We know passing best from examples we may have seen or read about where very light skinned African Americans choose to identify as white, that is they can pass as white and not be detected. Or many LGBT people who choose to perform as straight in their public lives, something still common in the entertainment industry and in politics and other venues of public life. In both of these instances, the person is able to pass because their membership in a stigmatized group is not visible or not readily visible. It is also the case that people, usually women, who are not visibly fat, but who feel fat, who live as if they were fat, women on the boundary of obese who, for example, can buy clothes in the normal size range rather than so-called "plus-sizes," can pass as normal despite how they feel within themselves. I was in that group years ago, but never felt that I was passing.

Earlier I spoke of having spent years as a Good Fatty. As a Good Fatty I was managing my fat identity by covering, by accepting that I should not be fat and trying to cover my failure by always being in the process of trying to change, a perpetual state of atonement for the sin of being too big and too much.

Now I call myself fat. Not curvy. Not Rubenesque. Not zaftig or plump. Fat. I call myself fat. Just by calling myself fat, using that word unselfconsciously and without shame or apology, is movement away from being the Good Fatty. Just by calling myself fat, I break the silence. But there is more to coming out fat than that. While I made the decision thirty-five years ago to stop dieting, I never talked about it with friends. Nor did I speak up when conversation turned to talk of diets and dieting. I wasn't dieting but I wasn't willing to be public with having stepped out of being good, of forever being on the way to being thin. I was still covering, at least outwardly. Being the Good Fatty is acting as if we embrace body hatred, dieting, guilt, and shame and thus we can at least be on the fringes of membership in the "normal" world.

When I was a Good Fatty, I would delay buying major clothing items like a winter coat because of the hope, the belief, the desire that next year I would be smaller. In my closet, as in the closets of many fat women, I had things that I could no longer wear, but which I kept in the hope that next year, someday, I could again wear those skinny jeans or that now-too-tight skirt. Because that is the way to be good. Always be on the way to thin, no matter how distant thin may be. No matter how long or how many unsuccessful attempts there are between now and that ever-elusive goal weight.

As a Good Fatty I did everything I could through my behavior to apologize for being fat, for taking up too much space in the world. I mutely accepted without challenge that I should have to go to special stores for clothing, deal with rude remarks on the street, comments from "helpful" friends and family about how much they worried for me and fervently wished I would lose weight, that I would stop "letting myself go." I hid my anger at the insults disguised as concerns for my wellbeing, the endless suggestions for what I should do to lose weight. When a waiter once told me that I did not need dessert, I did not protest. Because as a fat person, I tacitly accepted that I needed policing to keep myself in check.

In my life, I have been on just about every kind of diet you can imagine, starting when I was nine years old. Counting calories, low fat, low carb, Weight Watchers, Diet Workshop, Metrecal (remember that stuff?), diet pills, I've tried them all. I wanted with all my heart to believe that all I had to do was find the right plan and somehow magically I would be normal, I would become thin.

I did lose weight. Losing weight is actually fairly easy and any of those methods produces weight loss. But inevitably every single time the weight would slowly come back and I would end up where I was before, but in a perverse twist, a little heavier than when I started. I only stopped gaining weight when I stopped trying to lose weight. As Arya Sharma, a leading obesity researcher, put it:

> I often joke that the easiest way to gain 25 lbs. is to lose 20! Unfortunately, this may not be much of a joke, as there is mounting evidence that intentional weight loss may indeed be an important driver of long-term weigh gain. (Sharma, 2011)

But stopping dieting is not coming out. It is an act of rebellion, to be sure, but the rebel is always defined by that against which she rebels.

Coming out means letting go of the fantasy that there is a thin person inside waiting to get out and that she, not this fat me, is the real one. Coming out is to stop pretending to be trying to lose weight when I am not. Coming out means stopping defending how I eat or my health. Coming out is letting go of shame and embracing the body I have. Coming out is accepting myself, all of myself, fat and all.

Coming out means going in, inside myself and wrestling with the both/and-ness of it all. That yes, I come by this body honestly, but that doesn't mean it is all due to my biology. It means accepting that no matter how much I wrestle, the end of the match does not mean I will get thin. It means knowing that yes, anger and my relationship with my mother and all those other issues have played a role in the development of the body I have now. And in a sense, now I wear the results of having had those struggles for so long. Like the scars from any battle on those who have fought one, my body carries my scars, in the form of fat that won't go away.

Marion Woodman said of one of the patients she discusses in *Addiction to Perfection*,

> Rather than deal with the fat as fact, Ruth was trapped in unconscious identification with her large body. She had no ego with which to separate herself from whatever myth was being lived out through the fat. The reason she weighed 325 pounds was that she refused to accept the existential reality that her body was forced louder and louder to proclaim. (Woodman, 1982, p. 55)

I cannot agree. Ruth is fat and it does not matter, really, why she is fat, what the cause is. She is fat. And her body, being fat, is the trauma she experiences every day. It does matter how she feels, how she has been treated in her family and in the world, what she does with her anger. The rage, sorrow, fear, and pain she experiences from living in a body that is vilified, rejected, stigmatized—all of that is fruit for analysis. Ruth suffers from the ongoing trauma of being fat. And no amount of analysis with even the very best analyst can give her the thin body she, and it seems Marion Woodman, would like for her to have.

And that is perhaps the hardest thing, the most difficult part of coming out as fat. To identify with, really inhabit my fat body. Unconditionally.

Fat acceptance and fat activism—and for many, they are one and the same—generally follow principles articulated by Marilyn Wann, author of the book, *Fat! So?*. The assumption is that by claiming the word "fat" and embracing our fat bodies, somehow everything changes. This is how she puts it:

> Reclaiming the word fat is the miracle cure you've been looking for, the magic trick that makes all your worries about your weight disappear. Do you want to feel good about yourself? Silence your tormentors? Look better in miniskirts? Use the F-word. Dorothy made her wish come true by saying, "There's no place like home." Well, I'm not Glenda the Good Witch, but I'm here to tell you that all you have to do is say the magic word, fat. Say it loud, say it proud: Fat! Fat! Shake your belly three times and there you are, at home in your body, free from the guilt and the shame, the stress and starvation, and the self-hatred. (Wann, 1998, p. 18)

This very closely resembles the principles of cognitive behavioral therapy, that is, all one has to do to change feelings is to change thoughts. There is a degree of truth in that. Certainly working to stop hating my body was worthwhile. Choosing to use "fat" unselfconsciously defangs that word and it becomes just a descriptor, not an indictment. However just as cognitive behavioral therapy can only go so deep, so too with fat acceptance. That I accept my body as it is, that I accept and embrace my fatness does not in any way change the world around me. While accepting myself and my body is an essential first step, it is only a first step. It does nothing to detoxify the sea of judgment and prejudice I swim in.

Embracing fat acceptance gives a measure of dignity and a refuge from self-loathing but every day I confront the assumption that fat people have lost their self-control. And frighten others because there is such a premium placed on being thin, to the point of being a public obsession. Ask them and most people say they want to be slender, but this physical perfection is difficult to attain, harder hold on to and they fear losing control of it. Women, and men, can be on diets their whole lives. A fat person, particularly a fat person who seems at home with herself and her body is threatening. She of the jiggling flesh, the billowy hips, the soft folds of fat flies in the face of the washboard abs, botoxed faces, lean hard size zero of the supermodels held up to us all as icons of the ideal. Fear and unhappiness gets projected onto people who are bigger and that too often translates into abuse and attacks. In attacking fat people, the person terrified of the security of her grip on her own body disassociates herself from what she fears the most—getting fat. In this time of war on obesity, the fat person is the enemy and wears, obvious for all to see, the very thing that many fear will befall them if rigid control is not maintained. The fat person becomes the example of what no one should be. Many believe fat people are really thin people who have let themselves go, have fallen for the seduction of food. We are failed citizens. No matter what I do, no matter how I am able to be with myself, the reality is that there is more going on than simply how I feel in and about my body. In other words, when I leave the comfort of my home I have to deal with not only my own feelings but also my feelings in response to how others respond and react to me and to my body. As Samantha Moore puts it,

> I AM my body, and this understanding is always informed by cultural imaginings about bodies. My body and fat and my self are inextricably bound up in producing and reproducing my identity, which is always already corporeal. (Murray, 2005b, p. 276)

Coming out as fat is a process, not an event. Marion Woodman is wrong about some things but she is right about this:

> ... if we are to find our own truth, we have to go into our darkness alone and stay with our inner process until we find our own healing archetypal pattern ... It takes great courage to break with one's past history and stand alone. (Woodman, 1982, p. 28)

Each of us must find her own way through all of what fat represents in our lives, both physically and emotionally, and face into its complexity to find that healing space. Perhaps most importantly, break our silence and tell our stories.

I have known for some time that I stand a bit outside segments of the fat acceptance/fat activism world because I am aware of my ambivalence about my body. It was a relief to me to read Samantha Murray expressing some of the same ambivalence that I feel. I don't believe those fat activists who write about loving their bodies, all of their bodies. I don't believe it because I know it is more difficult than they make it sound. I know because I can be sailing along safe and sound in my fat acceptance, pleased with myself for how far I have come, and then I catch a glimpse of myself in a window or a photograph taken when I am off guard and like a squall coming up on an otherwise calm summer day, shame washes over me and I want to hide from view. A bubble of the shame that continues to reside in my fat is released because of what I see or some remark or something I read and it bubbles to the surface and floods over me.

I know that there are very few pictures of me. Now I wish there were more of me with my kids when they were little but I couldn't stand my own image so I avoided being in the frame. That my former husband did not cast a loving eye on me was all too apparent in the ways he photographed me and it made me feel ashamed so there are not many photos of me from those years. And of course, there are my arms, my arms that I still cannot comfortably bare in summer. Fat acceptance makes me support the right to bare fat arms, but so far, I cannot overcome my own resistance to doing so, even as I applaud others who do.

Now and then I run across a sentence buried deep inside something written by one of the writers in fat studies, a sentence confessing that she too has these moments of losing all that brave acceptance and feeling overwhelmed with the weight of her deviance and then I realize I am not alone in my ambivalence. I am split—I am the fat lady who sings, who is eager to tell her story and I am also anxious and gripped by this complex. I have learned over the last sixty-three years that I cannot be beautiful, not like slender women are. I cannot be one with women who are not fat because we inhabit different worlds even when we are sitting next to each other and no matter how conscious I become, I cannot change those messages that still bombard me everywhere I look. I can't pretend to be happy about being fat, because I am not. I can't pretend that I don't wish there were a safe way for me to have a different body, because I do wish that, or I did—now I know that sagging skin would make me feel even worse than my fat arms do. In a way what I have done is accept this as the body I have and done the work to make peace with it somehow and that is not the same as loving being fat. I care for my body as lovingly as I know how and that is not the same as loving my body.

A friend who read an earlier version of this chapter indicated surprise that I have not completely escaped from this complex. I had to say to her that of course I haven't. How could I? What I have done is broken the silence, engaged in telling my story, telling it again and again because so long as I and other fat women are silent, we maintain our own stigmatization. But just as for anyone with a trauma history, the memory of the trauma never goes away. What changes is the intensity of the response to that memory, intensity that diminishes as memory is allowed, as feeling is allowed.

REFERENCES

1 Boring Old Man. (2013). on history 1. http://1boringoldman.com/index. php/2013/01/25/on-history-1/ [last accessed 23 July 2016].

Adams, M. V. (1988). African American dreaming and the beast of racism the cultural unconscious in Jungian analysis. *Psychoanalytic Psychology*, 19(1): 182–198.

Alexander, C. (2008). Depression after bariatric surgery: triggers, identification, treatment, and prevention. http://bariatrictimes.com/ depression-after-bariatric-surgery-triggers-identification-treatment-and-prevention/ [last accessed 21 July 2016].

American Heart Association. (2014). Overweight in children. www.heart. org/HEARTORG/HealthyLiving/HealthyKids/ChildhoodObesity/ Overweight-in-Children_UCM_304054_Article.jsp#.Vv_Q6sca24I. [last accessed 2 August 2016].

American Psychological Association. Briefing series on the role of psychology in health care: Adult obesity. www.apa.org/health/briefs/adult-obesity.pdf [last accessed 15 August 2014].

American Psychological Association. (2012). APA to establish treatment guideline panels for obesity and PTSD. www.apa.org/science/about/ psa/2012/04/obesity-ptsd.aspx [last accessed 26 July 2016].

American Psychological Association. (2014). Psychologists' role in preventing and treating obesity though the lifespan. *APA Access*. www.apa.

org/pubs/newsletters/access/2014/04-15/treating-obesity.aspx. [last accessed 2 August 2016].

American Society of Plastic Surgeons. (2014a). American society of plastic surgeons reports 15.1 million cosmetic procedures in 2013; marks fourth consecutive year of growth. www.plasticsurgery.org/news/2014/ plastic-surgery-procedures-continue-steady-growth-in-us.html.

American Society of Plastic Surgeons. (2014b). Plastic surgery statistics report. Retrieved from www.plasticsurgery.org/Documents/news-resources/statistics/2013-statistics/cosmetic-procedures-national-trends-2013.pdf [last accessed 21 July 2016].

(ARAS), A. F. R. I. A. S. (2010). *The Book of Symbols: Reflections on Archetypal Images*. Cologne, Germany: Taschen Books.

Austin, G. L., Ogden, L. G., & Hill, J. O. (2011). Trends in carbohydrate, fat, and protein intakes and association with energy intake in normal-weight, overweight, and obese individuals: 1971–2006. *American Journal of Clinical Nutrition, 11*: 836–843.

Bacon, L. (2010). Thin privilege. http://lindabacon.org/HAESbook/pdf_files/HAES_Thin%20Privilege.pdf [last accessed 28 January 2015].

Bacon, L. (2012). The HAES® files: Obamacare's misfire on weight—new workplace provisions that deserve a pink slip. http://healthateverysizeblog.org/2012/07/10/the-haes-files-obamacare-misfire-on-weight-new-workplace-provisions-that-deserve-a-pink-slip/ [last accessed 17 July 2014].

Balsam, R. (2012). *Women's Bodies in Psychoanalysis*. New York, NY: Taylor and Francis.

Bennett, J. (2014). The gaze. In: *Voyages in Psychotherapy*. http:// voyagesinpsychotherapy.com/the-gaze/ [last accessed 20 August 2014].

Bennett, W. A., & Gurin, J. (1983). *The Dieter's Dilemma*. New York, NY: Basic Books.

Bias, S. (2014). Good fatty archetypes. http://stacybias.net/2014/06/12-good-fatty-archetypes/ [last accessed 1 October 2015].

Big Liberty (2011). Harvest the fatties as horse meat, and other gems of the moral panic [Web log post]. https://bigliberty.wordpress.com/2011/09/23/harvest-the-fatties-as-horse-meat-and-other-gems-of-the-moral-panic/ [last accessed 4 August 2016].

Bloom, C. (1994). Preface. Eating problems: a feminist psychoanalytic treatment model. In: C. Bloom, A. Gitter, S. A., Gutwill, L. S., Kogel, L., & L. Zaphiropoulis (Eds.), *Eating Problems: A Feminist Psychoanalytic Treatment Model* (pp. xi–xvi). New York, NY: Basic Books.

Blue, L. (2007). Obesity is contagious, study finds. http://content.time.com/time/health/article/0,8599,1646997,00.html [last acccessed 8 April 2013].

Bogart, L. (2013). I choose to be fat. http://www.salon.com/2013/07/25/ i_choose_to_be_fat/ [last accessed 21 July 2016].

Borero, N. (2012). *Killer Fat: Media, Medicine, and Morals in the American "Obesity Epidemic"*. New Brunswick, NJ: Rutgers University Press.

Bromberg, P. (2013). *Awakening the Dreamer: Clinical Journeys*. New York, NY: Taylor and Francis.

Brown, L. (1989). *Fat Oppression and Psychotherapy: A Feminist Perspective*. New York, NY: Haworth Press.

Bryant, T. (1981). Review: Woodman, Marion. The owl was a baker's daughter: obesity, anorexia nervosa, and the repressed feminine. *The San Francisco Jung Institute Library Journal*, 3(1): 27–36.

Burka, J. (2001). The therapist's body in reality and fantasy a perspective from an overweight therapist. In: B. Gerson (Ed.), *The Therapist as a Person: Life Crises, Life Choices, Life Experiences, and Their Effects on Treatment* (pp. 255–276). New York, NY: Routledge.

CaliforniaHealthline. (2004). Obesity second leading cause of preventable U.S. deaths, CDC study finds. www.californiahealthline.org/ articles/2004/3/10/obesity-second-leading-cause-of-preventable-us-deaths-cdc-study-finds [last accessed 28 November 2014].

Callan, G. M. (2004). The scapegoat complex: archetypal reflections on a culture of severance. http://midline.net/nfp/PDFs/Callan.pdf [last accessed 20 June 2014].

Campos, P., Saguy, A., Ernsberger, P., Oliver, E., & Gaesser, G. (2006). The epidemiology of overweight and obesity: public health crisis or moral panic? *International Journal of Epidemiology*, 35(1): 55–60.

Casazza, K., Fontaine, K. R., Astrup, A., Birch, L. L., Brown, A. W., Bohan Brown, M. M., et al. (2013). Myths, presumptions, and facts about obesity. *New England Journal of Medicine, 368*: 446–454.

Chambers, E. (Producer) & Philips, L. (Director). (1973). *The Girl Most Likely to …* [Motion Picture] USA: ABC Circle Films.

Cooper, C. (2007). *Headless fatties. London.* http://charlottecooper.net/ publishing/digital/headless-fatties-01-07 [last accessed 21 July 2016].

Chernin, K. (1994). *The Obsession: Reflections on the Tyranny of Slenderness*. New York, NY: Harper Perennial.

Chicago Tribune. FDA approves stomach-draining obesity treatment. www.chicagotribune.com/news/ct-fda-approves-stomach-draining-obesity-treatment-20160615-story.html [last accessed 14 June 2016].

Christakis, N. A., & Fowler, J. H. (2007). The spread of obesity in a large social network over 32 years. *New England Journal of Medicine*, 357: 370–379.

Cixous, H. (1976). The laugh of the medusa. *Signs*, 1: 875–893.

Cohen, S. (1973). *Folk Devils and Moral Panics*. St. Albans, UK: Paladin.

Craighead, M. (1986). *The Mother's Songs: Images of God the Mother*. Yahweh, New Jersey: Paulist Press.

Cunningham, E. (2014). Designers won't dress plus-size celebs. http:// www.thedailybeast.com/articles/2014/06/06/it-s-not-just-us-designers-won-t-dress-plus-size-celebs-either.html [last accessed 26 July 2016].

Darlington, B. (2009). The epidemic of obesity in contemporary american culture: A Jungian reflection. *Quadrant: The Journal of the C.G. Jung Foundation, 39*(1): 67–85.

Downey, M. (2015). The putative 104 causes of obesity update. www.downeyobesityreport.com/2015/10/the-putative-104-causes-of-obesity-update/[last accessed 29 February 2016].

Drell, W. (1988). Countertransference and the obese patient. *American Journal of Psychotherapy, 42*(1): 77–85.

Edison, L. T. (1994). *Women En Large: Images of Fat Nudes.* San Francisco: Books in Focus.

Ellis, C., Adams, T., & Bochner, A. (2010). Autoethnography: an overview. *Forum Qualitative Sozialforschung/Forum: Qualitative Social Research.* www.qualitative-research.net/index.php/fqs/article/view/1589/3095%3Cbr [last accessed 2 August 2016].

Engber, D. (2012). Fuzzy and Fizzy: The contested science behind Bloomberg's ban on large-sized sodas. www.slate.com/articles/health_and_science/science/2012/06/bloomberg_bans_large_sized_soda_the_science_behind_the_decision_.html [last accessed 2 August 2016].

Estes, C. P. (1992). *Women Who Run With the Wolves.* New York, NY: Basic Books.

Farrell, E. Obesity: how can we understand it? www.psychoanalysis-and-therapy.com/human_nature/free-associations/farrellob.dwt. [last accessed 10 May 2013].

Ferdman, R. (2015). Why diets don't work: Nobody has willpower. www.chicagotribune.com/lifestyles/health/ct-why-diets-dont-work-20150504-story.html#page=1 [last accessed 21 July 2016].

Ferguson, F. (2014). Shameless. http://healthateverysizeblog.org/tag/embodiment/ [last accessed 21 July 2016].

Filipovic, J. (2011). Why garment sizing is a social class issue. http://www.alternet.org/story/150743/why_garment_sizing_is_a_social_class_issue [last accessed 21 July 2016].

Fitzgerald, E. (2015). 5 baffling lies society told you about fat people. www.cracked.com/article_22964_5-baffling-lies-society-told-you-about-fat-people.html. [last accessed 2 August 2016].

Foucault, M. (1980). The eye of power. In: C. Gordon (Ed.), *Power/Knowledge: Selected Interviews and Other Writings 1972–1977 by Michel Foucault* (pp. 146–155). Sussex, UK: Harvester Press.

Foucault, M. (1995). *Discipline and Punish: The Birth of the Prison* (A. M. S. Smith, Trans.). New York, NY: Vintage Books.

Goffman, E. (1963). *Stigma: Notes on the Management of Spoiled Identity*. Englewood Cliffs, NJ: Prentice-Hall.

Goode, E., & Nachman, Ben-Yehuda. (1994). *Moral Panics: The Social Construction of Deviance*. Cambridge, MA: Blackwell.

Green, S. (2010). Embodied female experience through the lens of imagination. *Journal of Analytical Psychology, 55*: 339–360.

Greene, A. (2001). Conscious mind—unconscious body. *Journal of Analytical Psychology, 46*: 565–590.

Guntrip, H. (1969). *Schizoid Phenomena, Object-Relations and the Self*. New York, NY: International Universities Press.

Gutwill, S. (1994a). Women's eating problems: social context and the internalization of culture. In: C. Bloom, A. Gitter, S. Gutwill, & L. Zaphiropoulis (Eds.), *Eating Problems: A Feminist Psychoanalytic Treatment Model* (pp. 1–27). New York, NY: Basic Books.

Gutwill, S. (1994b). Transference and countertransference issues: the impact of social pressures on body image and consciousness. In: C. Bloom, A. Gitter S. Gutwill, & L. Zaphiropoulis, (Eds.), *Eating Problems: A Feminist Psychoanalytic Treatment Model* (pp. 144–171). New York, NY: Basic Books.

Hainer, V., & Aldhoon-Hainerová, I. (2013). Obesity paradox does exist. *Diabetes Care, 36*: 276–281.

Hammerman, S. (2013). Multifaith weight loss: the problem of fat, the promise of peace. http://religiondispatches.org/multifaith-weight-loss-the-problem-of-fat-the-promise-of-peace/ [last accessed 22 July 2016].

Healy, M. (2012). Obese adults should get counseling, federal task force says. www.latimes.com/nation/la-sci-obesity-screening-20120622-story.html [last accessed 22 July 2016].

Herman, C. P., & Polivy, J. (1980). Restrained eating. In: A. J. Stunkard (Ed.), *Obesity* (pp. 208–224). Philadelphia: Saunders.

Heska, S. (2001). Is obesity a disease? *International Journal of Obesity and Related Metabolic Disorders, 25*: 1401–1404.

Heuer, G. M. (2012). *"In My Flesh I Shall See God": Body and Psyche in Analysis*. London: Guild of Pastoral Psychology.

Hopcke, R. (1988). Jung and homosexuality: a clearer vision. *Journal of Analytical Psychology, 33*(1): 65–80.

Hopcke, R. (1989). *Jung, Jungians and Homosexuality*. Boston, MA: Shambala Publications.

Hughes, V. (2013). The big truth. www.nature.com/news/the-big-fat-truth-1.13039 [last accessed 22 July 2016].

Jackson, S., Steptoe, A., Beeken, R., Kivimaki, M., & Wardle, J. (2014). Psychological changes following weight loss in overweight and obese adults: a prospective cohort study. *PLOS/ONE*. http://dx.doi.org/10.1371/journal.pone.0104552 [last accessed 21 July 2016].

Johns, D. M. Disconnected? www.slate.com/articles/health_and_science/science/2011/07/disconnected.html [last accessed 21 July 2016].

Jung, C. G. (1933). *Modern Man in Search of a Soul*. New York, NY: Harcourt Brace and World.

Jung, C. G. (1966). General problems of psychotherapy. Fundamental questions of psychotherapy. In: G. Adler, & R. F. C. Hull, (Eds.), *Vol. 16: The Practice of Psychotherapy* (pp. 53–75). Princeton, NJ: Princeton University Press.

Jung, C. G. (1970). Woman in europe. In: G. Adler, & R. F. C. Hull (Eds.), *Vol. 10. Civilization in Transition* (pp. 113–133). Princeton, NJ: Princeton University Press

Jung, C. G. (1976a). Answer to Job. In: G. Adler, & R.F.C. Hull, (Eds.), *Vol. 11. Psychology and Religion: West and East* (pp.355–470). Princeton, NJ: Princeton University Press.

Jung, C. G. (1976b). The Tavistock lectures: on the theory and practice of analytical psychology. Lecture 1. In: G. Adler, & R.F.C. Hull (Eds.), *Vol. 18. The Symbolic Life* (pp. 1–35). Princeton, NJ: Princeton University Press.

Kaiser Health News (2009). CDC downscales mortality risk from obesity. http://khn.org/morning-breakout/dr00029473/ [last accessed 16 May 2014].

Kalsched, D. (1996). *The Inner World of Trauma: Archetypal Defenses of the Personal Spirit*. New York, NY: Routledge.

Kalsched, D. (1997). Hermes-Mercurius and the self-care system in cases of early trauma. In: S. Marlon (Ed.), *Fire in the Stone: The Alchemy of Desire* (pp. 94–124). Wilmette, IL: Chiron Publications.

Keen, S. Till the fat lady sings. http://samkeen.com/mini-stories/till-the-fat-lady-sings/ [last accessed 20 May 2015].

Kimbles, S. (2004). A cultural complex operating in the overlap of clinical and cultural space. In: T. Singer & S. Kimbles (Eds.), *The Cultural Complex: Contemporary Jungian Perspectives on Psyche and Society* (pp. 198–211). New York, NY: Routledge.

Kolata, G. (2005). Some extra heft may be helpful, new study says. www.nytimes.com/2005/04/20/health/20fat.html [last accessed 22 July 2016].

Kolata, G. (2007). Study says obesity can be contagious. www.nytimes.com/2007/07/25/health/25cnd-fat.html?_r=0 [last accessed 22 July 2016].

Krupnik, E. (2013). Tim Gunn: fashion seems to end at a size 12. www.huffingtonpost.com/2013/08/23/tim-gunn-size_n_3799450.html?utm_hp_ref=style&ir=Style [last accessed 22 July 2016].

Kuchuck, S. (2013). *Clinical Implications of the Psychoanalyst's Life Experience: When the Personal Becomes Professional*. New York, NY: Routledge.

Leach, K. (2009). *The Overweight Patient: A Psychological Approach to Understanding and Working with Obesity*. Philadelphia, PA: Jessica Kingsley Publishers.

Lebesco, K. (2010). Fat panic and the new morality. In: J. K. Metzl & A. Kirkland (Eds.), *Against Health: How Health Became the New Morality* (pp. 72–82). New York, NY: New York University Press.

Lewis, C. S. (1985). *Till We Have Faces*. New York, NY: Harcourt Brace Jovanovich.

Lockhart, R. (2012). *Words As Eggs: Psyche in Language and Clinic*. Seattle, WA: The Lockhart Press.

Lovejoy, A. O. (1976). *The Great Chain of Being: A Study of the History of an Idea*. Cambridge, MA: Harvard University Press.

Luckett, S. (2014). YoungGiftedandFat: performing transweight identities. *The Journal of American Drama and Theatre*. http://jadtjournal. org/2014/05/30/younggiftedandfat-performing-transweight-identities/ [last accessed 23 July 2016].

Lupton, D. (2012). *Fat*. New York, NY: Routledge.

Mann, T., Tomiyama, A. J., Westling, E., Lew, A. M., Samuels, B., & Chatman, J. (2007). Medicare's search for effective obesity treatments: diets are not the answer. *American Psychologist, 62*: 220–233.

Meador, B. (2004). Light the seven fires—seize the seven desires. In: T. Singer & S. Kimbles (Eds.), *The Cultural Complex: Contemporary Jungian Perspectives on Psyche and Society* (pp. 171–184). New York, NY: Routledge.

Medilexicon. (2015). Definition of Ideal Body Weight. http://www.medilexicon.com/medicaldictionary.php?t=99797 [last accessed 31 October 2015].

Meleo-Erwin, Z. (2011). "A beautiful show of strength": weight loss and the fat activist self. *Health, 15*: 188–205.

Meltzer, M. (2015). Plus-size fashion moves beyond the muumuu. www. nytimes.com/2015/01/01/fashion/plus-size-fashion-moves-beyond-the-muumuu.html [last accessed 23 July 2016].

Miller, B. (2010). Expressions of homosexuality and the perspective of analytical psychology. *Journal of Analaytical Psychology, 55*(1): 112–124.

Miller, B. H. (2010). A Sami healer's diagnosis: A case of embodied countertransference? In: R. Jones (Ed.), *Body, Mind and Healing After Jung: A Space of Questions* (pp. 145–159). London: Routledge.

Monick, E. (1987). *Phallos: Sacred Image of the Masculine*. Toronto: Inner City Books.

Moore, J. (2005). *Fat Girl: A True Story*. New York, NY: Plume.

Morris, J. (Producer), & Stanton, A. (Director). (2008). *WALL-E* [Motion Picture]. USA: Walt Disney Pictures.

Mosby's Medical Dictionary. Definition of Compulsive eating. http://medical-dictionary.thefreedictionary.com/Compulsive+Eating [last accessed 3 January 2015].

Moynihan, R. (2006). Obesity task force linked to WHO takes millions from drug firms. *British Medical Journal*, 332: 1412.

Mulvey, L. (1975). Visual pleasure and narrative cinema. *Screen* http://imlportfolio.usc.edu/ctcs505/mulveyVisualPleasureNarrativeCinema.pdf [last accessed 20 June 2015].

Murray, S. (2004). Locating aesthetics: Sexing the fat woman. *Social Semiotics*, 14: 237–247.

Murray, S. (2005a). (Un/be) coming out? Rethinking fat politics. *Social Semiotics*, 15: 153–163.

Murray, S. (2005b). Doing politics or selling out? Living the fat body. *Women's Studies: An Inter-disciplinary Journal*, 34: 265–277.

Murray, S. (2009). Women under/in control?: Embodying eating after gastric banding. *Radical Psychology: A Journal of Psychology, Politics and Radicalism*. www.radicalpsychology.org/vol8-1/murray.html.

Orbach, S. (2009). *Bodies (BIG IDEAS//small books)*. New York, NY: Picador.

Pace, G. (2006). Obesity bigger threat than terrorism? www.cbsnews.com/news/obesity-bigger-threat-than-terrorism/ [last accessed 23 July 2016].

Peay, P. (1992). An interview with Marion Woodman. *The San Francisco Jung Institute Library Journal*, 11(1): 5–23.

Pho, K. (2011). KevinMD's take, 28 September 2011. www.medpagetoday.com/Blogs/KevinMD/28770 [last accessed 2 August 2016].

Pollack, A. (2013). A.M.A. recognizes obesity as a disease. www.nytimes.com/2013/06/19/business/ama-recognizes-obesity-as-a-disease.html [last accessed 23 July 2016].

PR leap. (2013). Why are all the plastic surgeons men? www.prleap.com/pr/207181/why-are-all-the-plastic-surgeons-men [last accessed 24 July 2016].

Pressman, E. (Producer), & Stone, O. (Director). (1987). *Wall Street* [Motion Picture]. USA: Twentieth Century Fox.

Prose, F. (2003). *Gluttony* (Kindle ed.). New York, NY: Oxford University Press.

Quadrant. (n.d.) Journal Description. Retrieved from http://www.cgjungny.org/quadrant.html [last accessed August 2, 2016].

Quote Investigator. (2016). http://quoteinvestigator.com/2013/12/23/water-fish/ [last accessed 5 August 2016].

Richardson, S. A., Goodman, N., Hastorf, A. H., & Dornbusch, S. M. (1961). Cultural uniformity in reaction to physical disabilities. *American Sociological Review*, 26: 241–247.

Rosenblatt, R. (2001). Surgeon general takes stern stance on obesity. http://articles.latimes.com/2001/dec/14/news/mn-14788 [last accessed 23 July 2016].

Saguy, A. (2012). *What's Wrong with Fat?* (Kindle ed.). New York, NY: Oxford University Press.

Scott, H. W., & Law, D. H. (1969). Clinical appraisal of jejunoileal shunt in patients with morbid obesity. *American Journal of Surgery.*

Scott, H. W., Law, D. H., Sandstead, H. H., Lanier, V. C., & Younger, R. K. (1970). Jejunoileal shunt in surgical treatment of morbid obesity. *Annals of Surgery, 171:* 770–782.

Seacat, J. D., Dougal, S. C., & Roy, D. (2014). A daily diary assessment of female weight stigmatization. *Journal of Health Psychology, 21*(2): 228–240.

Selling, K. (2013). http://fatbodypolitics.tumblr.com/post/48892898729/when-it-comes-to-dressing-myself-i-live-by-a-very [last accessed 19 March 2014].

Sharma, A. (2011). Will losing weight make you fat? http://www.drsharma.ca/obesity-will-losing-weight-make-you-fat [last accessed August 2, 2016].

Sharma, A. (2013). Obesity myth: dieting is the best way to control your weight. www.drsharma.ca/obesity-myth-dieting-is-the-best-way-to-control-your-weight.html [last accessed 20 May 2015].

Sherman-Meyer, C. (2015). What's fat got to do with it? On different kinds of losses and gains in the analytic relationship, *Psychoanalytic Inquiry: A Topical Journal for Mental Health Professionals, 35:* 271–280.

Sieff, D. (2009). Confronting death mother: an interview with Marion Woodman. *Spring: A Journal of Archetype and Culture, 81:* 177–199.

Singer, T. (2004). The cultural complex and archetypal defenses of the group spirit. In: T. Singer & S. Kimbles (Eds.), *The Cultural Complex: Contemporary Jungian Perspectives on Psyche and Society* (pp. 12–33). New York, NY: Routledge.

Singer, T., & Kaplinsky, C. (2010). The cultural complex. http://aras.org/sites/default/files/docs/00042SingerKaplinsky.pdf [last accessed 2 August 2016].

Singer, T., & Kimbles, S. (Eds.). (2004). *The Cultural Complex: Contemporary Jungian Perspectives on Psyche and Society.* New York, NY: Routledge.

Smith, D. (2004). Demonizing fat in the war on weight. www.nytimes.com/2004/05/01/arts/demonizing-fat-in-the-war-on-weight.html. [last accessed 2 August 2016].

Sourcewatch. (2015). F. Xavier Pi-Sunyer. www.sourcewatch.org/index.php/F._Xavier_Pi-Sunyer [last accessed 5 May 2015].

Spence, L. White space, black space. www.busboysandpoets.com/blog/white-space-black-space [last accessed 28 December 2013].

Stevens Sullivan, B. (2009). *The Mystery of Analytical Work: Weavings from Jung and Bion*. New York, NY: Routledge.

Stump, S. (2016). Cheryl Tiegs criticizes SI for full-figured Ashley Graham cover: "I don't think it's healthy". www.today.com/health/cheryl-tiegs-criticizes-si-full-figured-ashley-graham-cover-i-t76356 [last accessed 24 July 201].

Stunkard, A. J. W. (1996). *Obesity: Theory and Therapy* (2nd ed.). New York, NY: Raven Press.

Sue, D. W. (2010). Microaggressions, marginality, and oppression: An introduction. In: D. Sue (Ed.), *Microaggressions and Marginality: Manifestation, Dynamics, and Impact* (pp. 3–23). Hoboken, NJ: John Wiley & Sons Inc.

Susman, E. (2014). Survey: nurses harsh on overweight patients. www.medpagetoday.com/MeetingCoverage/AANP/46428 [last accessed 30 June 2014].

Sutin, A. R., Stephan, Y., & Terracciano, A. (2015). Weight discrimination and risk of mortality. *Psychological Science, 26*: 1803–1811.

The American Congress of Obstetricians and Gynecologists. (2014). Ethical issues in the care of the obese woman. www.acog.org/Resources_And_Publications/Committee_Opinions/Committee_on_Ethics/Ethical_Issues_in_the_Care_of_the_Obese_Woman [last accessed 21 July 2016].

The Aspire Assist. http://aspirebariatrics.com/about-the-aspireassist/ [last accessed 21 May 2015].

The Center for Consumer Freedom (2005). Life expectancy: another obesity myth debunked. www.consumerfreedom.com/2005/03/2768-life-expectancy-another-obesity-myth-debunked/ [last accessed 5 April 2015].

The Laidly Worm of Spindleston Heugh. www.sacred-texts.com/neu/eng/eft/eft34.htm [last accessed 14 July 2014].

The Lord's Table: A biblical approach to weight loss. 16 February 2014 www.settingcaptivesfree.com/courses/lords-table/

The Washington Post. (2001). Text: President Bush addresses the nation. www.washingtonpost.com/wpsrv/nation/specials/attacked/transcripts/bushaddress_092001.html [last accessed 24 July 2016].

ThinkProgress. (2012). Public health experts warn next generation may have shorter life span as a result of obesity. http://thinkprogress.org/health/2012/05/04/478249/obesity-life-expectancy/ [last accessed 23 July 2016].

Tintner, J. (2010). The incredible shrinking shrink. In: J. Petrucelli (Ed.), *Knowing, Not-Knowing and Sort-of-Knowing: Psychoanalysis and the Experience of Uncertainty: Psychoanalysis and the Experience of Uncertainty* (Kindle ed.) (pp. 281–295). London: Karnac.

Tomiyama, A. J., Hunger, J. M., Nguyen-Cuu, J., & Wells, C. (2016). Misclassification of cardiometabolic health when using body mass index categories in NHANES 2005-2012. *International Journal of Obesity*, 40: 883–886.

UC Davis Medical Center. (2011). UC Davis study shows that fast-food dining is most popular for those with middle incomes, rather than those with lowest incomes. www.ucdmc.ucdavis.edu/medicalcenter/ features/2011-2012/12/20111215_fast-food.html [last accessed 24 July 2016].

UCONN Rudd Center for Food Policy and Obesity. (2015). Rudd center archive of images. www.uconnruddcenter.org/press/image_gallery. aspx [last accessed 3 November 2015].

Van der Kolk, B. (2015). *The Body Keeps the Score: Brain, Mind, and Body in the Healing of Trauma* (Kindle ed.). New York, NY: Penguin Group.

Vartanian, L. R. (2010). "Obese people" vs "fat people": impact of group label on weight bias. *Eating and Weight Disorders*, 15: 195–198.

Von Franz, M. L. (1972). *The Feminine in Fairy Tales*. Dallas, TX: Spring.

Wann, M. (1998). *Fat!So? Because You Don't Have to Apologise for your Size*. Berkeley, CA: Ten Speed Press.

Weinstein, R. J. (2014). *Fat Kids: Truth and Consequences*. New York, NY: Beaufort Books.

Welsh, T. (2011). Healthism and the bodies of women: Pleasure and discipline in the war against obesity. *Journal of Feminist Scholarship*, 1: 33–48.

Widdecombe, L. (2014). The plus side: full-figured fashion gets a new look. www.newyorker.com/magazine/2014/09/22/bigger-better [last accessed 24 July 2016].

Wilchins, R. A. (1997). *Read My Lips: Sexual Subversion and the End of Gender*. Ithaca, NY: Firebrand Books.

Williams, T. T. (2012). *When Women Were Birds: Fifty-four Variations on Voice* (Kindle ed.). New York, NY: Farrar, Straus and Giroux.

Winograd, B. (2014). Black psychoanalysts speak. www.pep-web.org/ document.php?id=pepgrantvs.001.0001a [last accessed 24 July 2016].

Withers, R. (2003). *Controversies in Analytical Psychology* (Kindle ed.). New York, NY: Taylor and Francis.

Woodman, M. (1980). *The Owl Was a Baker's Daughter: Obesity, Anorexia Nervosa, and the Repressed Feminine*. Toronto: Inner City Books.

Woodman, M. (1982). *Addiction to Perfection*. Toronto: Inner City Books.

Woodman, M. (1985). *The Pregnant Virgin*. Toronto: Inner City Books.

Woodman, M. (1990). The body as the cultural unconscious. *New Perspectives: A quarterly Bulletin about Rolfing and Somatic Awareness*. www.davidladen.com/Newsletters/New_Perspectives_009.pdf. [last accessed 21 September 2016].

Woodman, M. (2004). Trauma and the death mother. http://iaap.org/congresses/barcelona-2004/trauma-and-the-death-mother.html   [last accessed 10 May 2014].

Word Spy. (2015). Definition of McMansion. http://wordspy.com/words/McMansion.asp. [last accessed 4 May 2015].

Worldometers. (2015). Overweight and weight loss statistics. www.worldometers.info/weight-loss/ [last accessed 23 July 2016].

Yale Rudd Center. (2009). Rudd brief: weight bias 2009. www.yaleruddcenter.org/resources/upload/docs/what/reports/RuddBriefWeightBias2009.pdf [last accessed 2 March 2013].

Yalom, I. (1989). The fat lady. In: *Love's Executioner, And Other Tales Of Psychotherapy* (pp. 94–123). New York, NY: Harper Perennial.

Young Eisendrath, P. (1987). The absence of black americans as jungian analysts. *Quadrant, 20*: 41–53.

Young Eisendrath, P. (2012). *Jung, Gender and Subjectivity in Psychoanalysis* (Kindle ed.). New York, NY: Taylor and Francis.

Zimmerman, E. (1981). *Elizabeth Zimmermann's Knitter's Almanac*. Mineola, NY: Dover Publications.

INDEX

For Product Safety Concerns and Information please contact our EU
representative GPSR@taylorandfrancis.com
Taylor & Francis Verlag GmbH, Kaufingerstraße 24, 80331 München, Germany